RENAL L[____]

CW01456342

COOKBOOK FOR BEGINNERS

Emery Beckett

Table of Contents

CHAPTER 1

Introduction

A kidney renal diet often referred to as a renal or kidney-friendly diet is a specialized eating plan designed to support individuals with kidney disease or those at risk of kidney problems. This diet is carefully structured to minimize the workload on the kidneys and reduce the accumulation of waste products and excess fluids in the body. It plays a crucial role in managing various stages of kidney disease, from mild to severe, and is an essential part of a comprehensive kidney disease management plan.

The primary objective of a kidney renal diet is to maintain the overall health and function of the kidneys by carefully controlling the intake of certain nutrients, including sodium, potassium, phosphorus, and protein. This dietary approach helps to alleviate the burden on the kidneys and mitigate the symptoms and complications associated with kidney disease, such as fluid retention, electrolyte imbalances, and high blood pressure.

Key components of a kidney renal diet include:

- Sodium Restriction: Limiting sodium intake is essential to manage blood pressure and reduce fluid retention. This means avoiding high-sodium processed foods and using alternative herbs and spices for flavor.
- Potassium Management: Controlling potassium is vital, as high levels can lead to heart irregularities. The diet typically includes recommendations to limit high-potassium foods.
- Phosphorus Control: Kidneys with reduced function may struggle to regulate phosphorus levels in the blood. A renal diet often involves restricting high-phosphorus foods and using phosphate binders.
- Protein Adjustment: Protein consumption may be adjusted based on the stage of kidney disease. A lower-protein diet can help reduce the accumulation of waste products in the blood.
- Fluid Intake Monitoring: Patients are often advised to manage their fluid intake to prevent fluid overload, which can strain the kidneys and lead to edema and hypertension.
- Caloric Balance: Maintaining a healthy body weight and addressing any underlying conditions like diabetes is also a key aspect of a kidney renal diet.

A well-balanced kidney renal diet is typically individualized, taking into account the patient's stage of kidney disease, nutritional requirements, and any coexisting medical conditions. Individuals are frequently encouraged to collaborate closely with a registered dietitian or a healthcare expert in devising a personalized meal plan that caters to their unique requirements. These dietary adjustments have the potential to decelerate the advancement of kidney disease, relieve associated symptoms, and enhance the overall quality of life for individuals dealing with kidney-related health concerns.

Renal failure, also known as kidney failure, is a medical state that occurs when the kidneys are not capable to execute their vital functions adequately. To understand renal failure, it's essential to first grasp the anatomy and function of the kidneys.

Anatomy of the Kidneys:

The shape of kidney looks like bean and it is located on either side of the spine, just under the ribcage. It is a part of urinary system and it has complex structure with several distinct regions, each playing a crucial role in their function.

- Renal Cortex: The outermost layer of the kidney is referred to as the renal cortex and is abundant in nephrons, which serve as the fundamental functional components of the kidneys. Nephrons are dependable for filtering blood and regulating the concentration of various substances in the body.
- Renal Medulla: Below the cortex lies the renal medulla, which contains structures called renal pyramids. These pyramids have a role in concentrating urine.
- Renal Pelvis: The structure of renal pelvis looks like fennel in the center of kidney, where urine from the nephrons collects. From here, urine flows into the ureter and eventually into the bladder for elimination.
- Renal Arteries and Veins: The kidneys are highly vascular organs, receiving a

significant portion of the cardiac output. The kidneys receive their blood supply from the renal arteries, and once this blood is filtered, it is transported away by the renal veins.

Renal Function:

The major function of the kidney is to maintain the internal environment of the body by performing various essential tasks, including:

- Filtration: The nephrons filter waste products, excess ions, and water from the blood. This filtered fluid, known as filtrate, is the starting point for urine formation.
- Reabsorption: After filtration, the nephrons reabsorb necessary substances such as glucose, sodium, and water, returning them to the bloodstream to maintain essential bodily functions.
- Secretion: The kidneys also secrete substances like hydrogen ions and potassium into the filtrate, helping to regulate the pH of the body and electrolyte balance.
- Excretion: The final step in urine formation involves excreting the remaining waste products and excess substances as urine, which then travels through the urinary tract for elimination.
- Regulation of Blood Pressure: Blood Pressure Regulation: Kidneys have a crucial role in the regulation of blood pressure, modulating blood volume and sodium concentration within the body.
- Erythropoiesis Regulation: They generate and secrete erythropoietin, a hormone that

prompts the bone marrow to generate red blood cells.

Types of Renal Failure:

Renal failure can be classified into two main types: acute and chronic.

- Acute Renal Failure (ARF): It is also called acute kidney injury (AKI), ARF is a sudden and severe decline in kidney function. It can result from various causes, including dehydration, severe infections, toxins, or a sudden drop in blood flow to the kidneys. If identified and treated promptly, ARF is often reversible.
- Chronic Renal Failure (CRF): Chronic renal failure, or chronic kidney disease (CKD), is a long-term condition characterized by a gradual and irreversible loss of kidney function. It typically develops over a period of months or years and can result from various underlying conditions, including hypertension, diabetes, or recurrent kidney infections.

Symptoms and Indicators:

The manifestations and markers of renal failure may differ based on its classification and progression. Typical indicators encompass:

- Fatigue
- Swelling in the legs, ankles, or feet
- Shortness of breath
- Nausea and vomiting
- Loss of appetite
- Changes in urine output or color
- High blood pressure
- Itching and skin rashes
- Muscle cramps and weakness
- Confusion and difficulty concentrating

Diagnosis and Treatment:

Diagnosing renal failure involves a combination of physical examination, medical history, Blood tests, and laboratory tests. For example, blood urea nitrogen (BUN) and serum creatinine are often used to assess kidney function.

Treatment for renal failure depends on its type and severity:

- Acute Renal Failure: Treatment aims to address the underlying cause and support kidney function. This may include managing fluid and electrolyte balance, optimizing blood pressure, and addressing any infections or toxins.
- Chronic Renal Failure: Managing chronic kidney disease involves controlling underlying conditions, such as diabetes or hypertension, and slowing the progression of kidney damage. In advanced stages, treatments like dialysis or kidney transplantation may be necessary.

Complications:

Untreated or poorly managed renal failure can direct to different complications, including:

- Fluid and electrolyte imbalances
- Metabolic acidosis
- Hypertension
- Anemia
- Bone and mineral disorders
- Cardiovascular disease
- Uremia (the buildup of waste products in the blood)

Prevention:

Preventing renal failure involves maintaining a healthy lifestyle and managing underlying medical conditions. Some key steps include:

- Staying hydrated
- Managing diabetes and hypertension
- Avoiding excessive use of medications that can harm the kidneys
- Monitoring kidney function through regular check-ups
- Following a balanced diet low in salt and processed foods

The kidneys are vital organs responsible for maintaining the body's internal balance by filtering blood, regulating fluid and electrolyte levels, and excreting waste products. Renal failure can be acute or chronic and has a wide range of causes and symptoms. Early diagnosis and suitable treatment are essential for managing the condition and preventing complications. Additionally, a healthy lifestyle and regular medical check-ups can help decrease the risk of developing renal failure.

Warning signs and early diagnosis of kidney failure

Early diagnosis of kidney failure is crucial to initiate timely treatment and prevent the progression of the condition. There are several warning signs and symptoms that may indicate the presence of kidney problems. These signs can be indicative of both acute and chronic kidney failure. It is significant to be aware of these warning signs and seek medical attention if you experience them. Here are some key warning signs and the diagnostic methods used to identify kidney failure:

Changes in Urination:

- Frequent Urination: An increased need to urinate, especially during the night, can be a sign of kidney dysfunction.
- Decreased Urination: A reduction in the volume of urine or oliguria (urinating less than normal) may signal kidney problems.

Changes in Urine Characteristics:

- Blood in Urine (Hematuria): The presence of blood in the urine may indicate kidney damage, infection, or kidney stones.
- Foamy or Bubbly Urine: Excessive foam or bubbles in the urine may be a sign of protein leakage from the kidneys (proteinuria), which is common in kidney disease.
- Dark Colored Urine: Dark or tea-colored urine can result from kidney issues or muscle breakdown.
- Swelling (Edema): Swelling in the face, hands, legs, or ankles, also known as edema, may occur due to fluid retention resulting from impaired kidney function.
- Fatigue and Weakness: Kidney failure can guide to anemia, which causes a decrease in the number of red blood cells and may result in fatigue and weakness.
- High Blood Pressure (Hypertension): Uncontrolled high blood pressure can damage the kidneys and is both a cause and consequence of kidney disease.
- Back Pain or Flank Pain: Pain in the lower back or sides (flank pain) can be a symptom of kidney problems, such as kidney stones or kidney infection.
- Nausea and Vomiting: Nausea, vomiting, and loss of appetite are common

symptoms in kidney disease, particularly in the advanced stages.

- Itching and Skin Rash: The increase of waste products in the blood due to kidney dysfunction can lead to itching and skin rashes.
- Metallic Taste in Mouth and Ammonia Breath: Uremia, a condition caused by the accumulation of waste products in the blood, can result in a metallic taste in the mouth and foul-smelling breath (ammonia odor).

Diagnostic Methods for Kidney Failure:

If you experience one or more of the warning signs mentioned above, it is important to consult a healthcare provider for a proper evaluation. The following diagnostic methods can help identify kidney failure:

- **Blood Tests:**
- Serum Creatinine: Elevated levels of serum creatinine can indicate impaired kidney function.
- Blood Urea Nitrogen (BUN): High BUN levels may also suggest kidney dysfunction.
- **Urine Tests:**
- Urine Analysis: Examination of a urine sample can reveal abnormalities such as proteinuria, hematuria, and the presence of cellular elements.
- **Imaging Studies:**
- Ultrasound: A renal ultrasound can provide images of the kidneys to assess their size and structure.

- CT Scan or MRI: These imaging techniques can offer more detailed views of the kidneys and help identify obstructions, tumors, or other structural issues.
- **Kidney Biopsy:**
- In some cases, a kidney biopsy may be performed to observe a small tissue sample from the kidney to determine the cause of kidney damage.
- **Glomerular Filtration Rate (GFR):**
- GFR is a calculated value based on serum creatinine levels and other factors. It helps determine the degree of kidney function. A lower GFR indicates reduced kidney function.
- **Medical History and Physical Examination:**
- Your healthcare provider will ask about your medical history and conduct a physical examination to look for signs of kidney problems.
- **Blood Pressure Measurement:**
- Regular monitoring of blood pressure is essential, as hypertension is both a risk factor for kidney disease and a potential consequence of kidney dysfunction.

Early diagnosis and intervention can help manage kidney problems effectively and prevent the progression to kidney failure. If you notice any warning signs or have risk factors for kidney disease (such as diabetes or hypertension), it is wise to ask a healthcare professional for a thorough evaluation and proper management.

Link between diet and management of renal failure

Diet plays an essential role in the management of renal failure, particularly in chronic kidney disease (CKD). A well-planned and balanced diet can help slow the progression of the disease, alleviate symptoms, and reduce the risk of complications. The link between diet and the management of renal failure is closely related to controlling various dietary components to ease the burden on the kidneys and maintain overall health. Here are key dietary considerations for managing renal failure:

Protein Intake:

Limiting protein intake is often necessary in advanced stages of CKD to reduce the accumulation of waste products in the blood. High-protein diets can strain the kidneys. Protein should be of high biological value and sourced from lean meats, poultry, fish, and dairy.

In the later stages, a healthcare provider may recommend a low-protein diet. Protein-restricted diets must be carefully monitored to prevent malnutrition.

Sodium (Salt) Restriction:

Reducing sodium intake helps manage blood pressure and fluid retention. High salt intake can exacerbate hypertension and swelling in individuals with renal failure.

Avoid processed and packaged foods, as they are frequently high in sodium. Choose fresh, whole foods and season dishes with herbs and spices instead of salt.

Phosphorus Control:

High levels of phosphorus in the blood can lead to bone and mineral disorders. Phosphorus intake should be limited, and phosphorus-binding medications may be prescribed.

Foods high in phosphorus include dairy products, nuts, seeds, and processed foods. It's essential to choose low-phosphorus alternatives.

Potassium Management:

Hyperkalemia (high potassium levels) is a concern in kidney failure. It can lead to heart rhythm disturbances.

Potassium intake may need to be restricted and potassium-rich foods like bananas, oranges, and potatoes should be consumed in moderation.

Fluid Restriction:

In advanced stages of CKD, fluid intake may need to be limited to prevent fluid overload and swelling. The recommended daily fluid allowance will be determined by a healthcare provider.

Caloric Adequacy:

Sufficient calorie intake is necessary to maintain energy levels and prevent muscle wasting. People with kidney failure often have a decreased appetite, so it's crucial to focus on nutrient-dense foods.

Healthy Fats:

Choose heart-healthy fats, such as those found in avocados, nuts, and olive oil, while limiting saturated and trans fats. Fat intake is usually not restricted unless it's necessary for other medical conditions.

Calcium and Vitamin D:

Calcium and vitamin D supplements may be recommended to maintain bone health since kidney disease can affect the body's ability to use these nutrients properly.

Consultation with a Dietitian:

A registered dietitian who specializes in kidney disease can make a personalized meal plan based on an individual's specific needs and stage of kidney disease.

Monitoring Blood Levels:

Regular blood tests, for example, blood urea nitrogen (BUN), serum creatinine, potassium, phosphorus, and calcium levels, help determine the effectiveness of dietary modifications and guide further adjustments.

Limiting Phosphate Additives:

Processed and convenience foods often contain phosphate additives. Checking food labels for additives like phosphoric acid and other phosphate-based ingredients can help reduce phosphorus intake.

Limiting High-Purine Foods:

High-purine foods, like organ meats and certain seafood, can lead to increased levels of uric acid in the blood, which may exacerbate kidney problems.

CHAPTER 2

Comprehensive guide to recommended foods, foods to limit and food to avoid

A comprehensive renal kidney diet, often recommended for individuals with kidney failure or chronic kidney disease (CKD), involves careful consideration of the types and amounts of foods consumed. The goal is to manage the condition, support kidney function, and prevent complications. Here's a guide to recommended foods, foods to limit, and foods to avoid for a renal kidney diet:

Recommended Foods:

- Premium Protein Sources: Skinless poultry, Lean meats, turkey, and chicken.
- Fish: Salmon, trout, herring, and other fatty fish rich in omega-3 fatty acids.
- Eggs: Egg whites or egg substitutes are lower in phosphorus than yolks.
- Low-Potassium Fruits: Apples, berries, grapes, and watermelon. These are lower in potassium compared to bananas, oranges, and melons. Cooking or leaching fruits can reduce their potassium content.
- Low-Phosphorus Vegetables: Green beans, cabbage, cauliflower, and peppers. These have lower phosphorus content compared to spinach, potatoes, and tomatoes. Boiling or soaking vegetables can help reduce their phosphorus content.
- Grains and Starches: White bread, white rice, pasta, and noodles. These are lower in potassium and phosphorus than whole grain and whole wheat options.
- Dairy Alternatives: Unenriched rice milk, almond milk, or coconut milk. These are lower in phosphorus compared to dairy milk. Choose low-phosphorus dairy products if you prefer traditional milk.
- Healthy Fats: Olive oil, canola oil, and avocado. These fats are heart-healthy and suitable for a renal diet.
- Herbs and Spices: Utilize herbs and spices such as oregano, thyme, basil and lemon zest to flavor dishes instead of salt.
- Low-Sodium Condiments: Low-sodium soy sauce, mustard, and vinegar can enhance the taste of foods without adding excessive salt.
- Low-Protein Foods: Cereals, pasta, and bread can be consumed in moderation, especially if protein intake is restricted.
- Berries and Cherries: Berries, particularly blueberries, and cherries are rich in antioxidants and may help reduce inflammation and improve kidney function.

Foods to Limit:

- Protein Sources: Limit high-protein foods like red meat, processed meats (sausages, bacon), and organ meats, as they can increase the burden on the kidneys.
- High-Potassium Fruits and Vegetables: Potassium should be limited but not completely avoided. Control portion sizes of high-potassium foods like bananas, oranges, potatoes, and tomatoes.

- Dairy Products: Choose low-phosphorus dairy products and consume them in moderation to manage phosphorus levels.
- Whole Grains: Limit whole grains, whole wheat products, and bran cereals, as they are higher in phosphorus.
- Nuts and Seeds: Limit or avoid nuts, seeds, and nut butters, as they are high in phosphorus and potassium.
- High-Potassium Beverages: Reduce the consumption of high-potassium beverages like orange juice and tomato juice.
- Processed Foods: Avoid or limit processed and convenience foods, as they often contain high levels of sodium and phosphorus.

Foods to Avoid:

- High-Sodium Foods: Processed meats, canned soups, and restaurant/fast food are often very high in sodium and should be avoided.
- High-Potassium Foods: Avoid high-potassium foods like dried fruits, bananas, and potatoes in their various forms.
- High-Phosphorus Foods: Phosphorus-containing additives in processed foods should be avoided. Check food labels for terms like "phos" or "phosphate."
- Excessive Sugar: Foods and beverages high in added sugars can contribute to health problems, so it's advisable to minimize sugar intake.
- Alcohol: Limit alcohol consumption, as excessive alcohol can harm the kidneys and interact with medications.

- Excessive Fluids: In advanced CKD, fluid intake may need to be restricted, so consult a healthcare provider for guidance.

Balance between protein, sodium and phosphorus:

Balancing protein, sodium, and phosphorus intake is crucial for a kidney failure diet, particularly in chronic kidney disease (CKD). Achieving the right balance helps manage symptoms, slow the evolution of kidney disease, and reduce the risk of complications. Here's how to strike the appropriate balance between these three nutrients:

Protein:

Protein is an essential nutrient that provides the body with amino acids for growth and maintenance. In kidney failure, protein intake needs to be moderated to reduce the burden on the kidneys and manage waste product buildup. The key is to ensure an adequate intake of high-quality protein while avoiding excessive consumption.

Recommendations for Protein Intake:

- High-Quality Protein Sources: Choose lean meats (chicken, turkey, fish), eggs (egg whites or egg substitutes), and dairy products. These are sources of high-quality protein with fewer waste products.
- Limit Red and Processed Meats: Red meat and processed meats (e.g., sausages, bacon) should be consumed in moderation due to their higher waste product content.
- Adequate but Controlled Protein: The typical protein requirement for individuals managing CKD is roughly 0.6 to 0.75 grams of protein per kilogram of body weight per day. It's essential to note that

these guidelines may fluctuate depending on an individual's unique situation, and it is advisable to consult with a healthcare provider or dietitian for personalized dietary recommendations.

- Consider Plant-Based Protein: Plant-based sources of protein, like tofu and legumes, can be included but should also be monitored for phosphorus content.

Sodium (Salt):

Sodium can contribute to fluid retention and high blood pressure, which can exacerbate kidney disease and its symptoms. Reducing sodium intake is essential for managing kidney failure.

Recommendations for Sodium Intake:

- Limit Processed and Packaged Foods: These have high levels of sodium. Opt for fresh, whole foods and cook at home when you want.
- Use Low-Sodium Alternatives: Replace regular table salt with low-sodium versions, and choose low-sodium condiments like soy sauce, mustard, and vinegar.
- Pay Attention to Food Labels: Examine nutritional labels to assess the sodium content and opt for items featuring reduced sodium levels.

Phosphorus:

Phosphorus is a mineral that can accumulate in the bloodstream when the kidneys are not functioning properly. High levels of phosphorus can lead to bone and mineral disorders.

Recommendations for Phosphorus Intake:

- Limit High-Phosphorus Foods: Avoid or limit high-phosphorus foods such as dairy products (especially aged cheeses), nuts, seeds, and whole grains.
- Phosphorus Binders: If phosphorus levels are difficult to control through diet alone, a healthcare provider may prescribe phosphorus-binding medications to reduce absorption.

Balancing Protein, Sodium, and Phosphorus:

- Balancing these nutrients in a renal diet can be challenging but is vital for overall kidney health. Here are some additional tips:
- Consult a Registered Dietitian: A dietitian specializing in renal nutrition can create a personalized meal plan that balances protein, sodium, and phosphorus according to an individual's specific needs and stage of kidney disease.
- Regular Monitoring: Regular blood tests are necessary to monitor levels of waste products, electrolytes, and minerals in the blood. This helps determine the effectiveness of dietary modifications and guide further adjustments.
- Stay Hydrated: Maintaining adequate fluid intake helps to wash out desecrate products from the body, but in advanced stages of CKD, fluid intake may need to be restricted. Consult a healthcare provider for guidance.
- Medication Management: Be aware of any medications prescribed by your healthcare provider, including phosphorus binders or

medications to control blood pressure. Adherence to medication regimens is essential.

PRAL (Potential Renal Acid Load): what it is and how to keep it monitored

The Potential Renal Acid Load (PRAL) is a measure used to assess the acid or alkaline nature of a person's diet and its potential impact on the body's acid-base balance. It is primarily relevant in the context of kidney health, bone health, and certain chronic diseases. PRAL estimates the potential renal acid load of a diet based on the dietary intake of specific minerals, primarily calcium, potassium, magnesium, and phosphorus.

Here's how PRAL works and how to keep it monitored:

How PRAL is calculated:

PRAL is calculated based on the acid-forming (acidic) or base-forming (alkaline) potential of various dietary components. Acid-forming components include sulfur-containing amino acids (e.g., methionine and cysteine) found in proteins, and phosphorus. Base-forming components include calcium, potassium, and magnesium.

The formula for calculating PRAL is:

PRAL (mEq/day) = 0.49 × protein (g/day) + 0.037 × phosphorus (mg/day) - 0.021 × potassium (mg/day) - 0.026 × magnesium (mg/day) - 0.013 × calcium (mg/day)

Interpretation of PRAL:

- Positive PRAL: A positive PRAL indicates an acid-forming diet. This means that the diet has the potential to increase the acidity of the body and may lead to acid-base imbalances.
- Negative PRAL: A negative PRAL indicates a base-forming diet. This diet is more alkaline and may help in neutralizing acid load in the body.

Monitoring and Managing PRAL:

Monitoring PRAL can be useful in certain clinical conditions, such as chronic kidney disease (CKD), osteoporosis, and metabolic acidosis.

Here's how to monitor and manage PRAL:

Consult a Dietitian: A registered dietitian specializing in renal nutrition or bone health can help you assess your diet's PRAL and make necessary modifications based on your health condition and dietary preferences.

Balancing Acid-Forming and Alkalinizing Foods:

- To reduce PRAL, consume more alkalinizing foods rich in calcium, potassium, and magnesium. These include fruits, vegetables, and certain dairy products.
- Limit acid-forming foods, especially those high in animal protein, phosphorus, and sulfur-containing amino acids, such as red meat, processed meats, and some grains.
- Control Protein Intake: While protein is essential, particularly in managing kidney disease, choosing high-quality protein sources that are lower in sulfur-containing amino acids can help maintain a better acid-base balance.
- Minimize Phosphorus Intake: Limit high-phosphorus foods, especially if you have kidney disease. These foods can

contribute to a positive PRAL. Phosphorus binders may be prescribed by a healthcare provider to control phosphorus levels in advanced CKD.

- Be Mindful of Calcium: Calcium can have an alkalinizing effect, so it's important to include calcium-rich foods in your diet. However, avoid excessive calcium supplementation, as it can have adverse effects on kidney health.

- Stay Hydrated: Staying well-hydrated helps flush out excess acids and maintain acid-base balance. However, in advanced CKD, fluid intake may need to be restricted, so follow your healthcare provider's recommendations.

- Regular Blood Tests: Periodic blood tests will help monitor acid-base balance, kidney function, and mineral levels in your body. Consult your healthcare provider for guidance on the frequency of these tests.

Avocado & Spinach Smoothie

Preparation time: 5 mins
Cooking time: 0 mins
Difficulty level: Easy
Serving: 1
PRAL: -14.2

Ingredients:

- 1 cup spinach leaves, should be fresh
- 1 cup almond milk
- Half avocado, should be ripe
- 1-2 tbsp honey

Instructions:

- Firstly, peel & pit the avocado. Place the honey, fresh spinach, avocado, & almond milk into the food processor. Mix & Mix.
- Serve!

Nutrition: Calories 300, Carbohydrate 40g, Fat 14g, Sugar 20g, Protein 4g,Potassium 600mg, Sodium 100mg, Phosphorus 100mg

Blueberry Oatmeal Muffins

Preparation time: 10 mins
Cooking time: 20 mins
Difficulty level: medium
Serving: 1
PRAL: -7.6

Ingredients:

- 1 cup rolled oats
- 1 cup fresh blueberries
- 1 cup whole wheat flour
- Two eggs
- 1 cup soy milk
- Half cup honey

Instructions:

- Firstly, preheat the oven to 350 degrees F.
- After this, line a muffin tin with paper liners.
- Add soy milk & rolled oats into the bowl & soak for 10 mins.
- Add honey & eggs in another bowl & toss together.
- Add soy mixture to the egg mixture & combine together.
- Put the mixture into the muffin tin.
- Bake for 18 to 20 mins.
- Enjoy!

Nutrition: Calories 160, Carbohydrate 33g, Fat 2g, Sugar 15g, Protein 4g,Potassium 160mg, Sodium 40mg, Phosphorus 120mg

Yogurt with Berries & Chia Seeds

Preparation time: 5 mins
Cooking time: 0 mins
Difficulty level: Easy
Serving: 1
PRAL: -2.5

Ingredients:

- 1 cup Greek yogurt, should be fat-free
- ½ cup mixed berries such as strawberries, blueberries, raspberries
- 1 tbsp chia seeds
- 1 to 2 tsp honey

Instructions:

- Add Greek yogurt into the mixing bowl.
- Add rinsed mixed berries to the Greek yogurt & mix well.
- Add chia seeds & honey & combine together.
- Enjoy!

Nutrition:

Calories 250, Carbohydrate 30g, Fat 3g, Sugar 20g, Protein 15g, Potassium 250mg, Sodium 100mg, Phosphorus 200mg

Oatmeal Pancakes with Blueberry Sauce

Preparation time: 10 mins
Cooking time: 10 mins
Difficulty level: Medium
Serving: 1
PRAL: -7.8

Ingredients:

- One cup oat flour
- Two eggs
- One cup almond milk
- One tsp butter, for grease
- Half cup blueberries
- 2 tbsp honey

Instructions:

- Add eggs, oat flour, & almond milk in a decent mixing bowl & mix together.
- Add fresh blueberries & mix together.
- Then, heat the griddle over intermediate heat.
- Apply some butter.
- Pour the batter for pancake & cook for 2-3 mins per side.
- Enjoy!

Nutrition:

Calories 260, Carbohydrate 35g, Fat 6g, Sugar 15g, Protein 9g, Potassium 200mg, Sodium 100mg, Phosphorus 150mg

Toast with Avocado & Cherry Tomatoes

Preparation time: 10 mins
Cooking time: 1 min
Difficulty level: Easy
Serving: 1
PRAL: -2.6

Ingredients:

- Two slices of whole-wheat bread
- 1 cup cherry tomatoes
- 1 tbsp olive oil
- 1 avocado, should be ripe
- Black pepper, as desired

Instructions:

- Firstly, toast the bread until crispy.
- Slice the avocado in half & remove the pit. Transfer the flesh into the medium bowl.
- Mash with a fork until creamy. Cut the tomatoes in half.
- Add pepper, olive oil, & cherry tomatoes into the bowl & mix together.
- Spread the mashed avocado onto the toasted bread.
- Top with olive oil mixture.
- Enjoy!

Nutrition:

Calories 300, Carbohydrate 36g, Fat 16g, Sugar 3g, Protein 7g,Potassium 600mg, Sodium 300mg, Phosphorus 150mg

Mixed Vegetable Frittata

Preparation time: 15 mins
Cooking time: 30 mins
Difficulty level: Medium
Serving: 1
PRAL: 3.9

Ingredients:

- 4 eggs
- ½ cup bell peppers, cut into little pieces
- ½ cup diced zucchini, cut into little pieces
- ½ cup tomatoes, diced
- ¼ cup onion, diced
- 1 cup spinach, chopped
- Black pepper, to taste
- Olive oil, for cooking

Instructions:

- Firstly, preheat the oven to 350 degrees F.
- Add olive oil into the skillet & heat it.
- Add onion & sauté it. Then, add zucchini & bell peppers & sauté it.
- Add chopped spinach & tomatoes & sauté for 2 mins.
- Add pepper & eggs in another bowl & mix together.
- Pour egg mixture over cooked veggies into the skillet & cook for a few mins.
- Put the skillet into the oven & cook for 15 to 20 mins.
- Enjoy!

Nutrition:

Calories 250, Carbohydrate 8g, Fat 12g, Sugar 3g, Protein 12g, Potassium 350mg, Sodium 300mg, Phosphorus 200mg

Quinoa & Red Fruits Porridge

Preparation time: 5 mins
Cooking time: 20 mins
Difficulty level: Easy
Serving: 1
PRAL: -2.1

Ingredients:

- ½ cup quinoa
- 1 cup mixed red fruits – strawberries, raspberries, & blueberries
- 1 cup soy milk
- 1-2 tbsp honey

Instructions:

- Run the quinoa under cold water.
- Add soy milk & rinsed quinoa into the saucepan & boil it.
- When boiled, decrease the heat to low & simmer for 15-20 mins.
- Rinse the red fruits under cold water. Then, cut into small pieces.
- Once the quinoa is cooked, remove it from the heat. Allow it to cool for one minute.
- Add honey & stir well.
- Add quinoa porridge into the bowl & top with sliced fruits.
- Serve!

Nutrition:

Calories 300, Carbohydrate 60g, Fat 6g, Sugar 15g, Protein 8g, Potassium 300mg, Sodium 300mg, Phosphorus 200mg

Whole Grain Crepes

Preparation time: 10 mins
Cooking time: 8 mins
Difficulty level: Easy
Serving: 1
PRAL: -7.4

Ingredients:

- 1 cup whole wheat flour
- 1 ½ cups almond milk
- Maple syrup, for topping

Instructions:

- Add almond milk & whole-wheat flour into the mixing bowl & mix well. Allow it to rest for 10-15 mins.
- Pour oil into the intermediate skillet & heat it. Pour the crepe batter into the middle & cook for 1-2 mins per side.
- Take out the crepe from the skillet.
- Drizzle with maple syrup.
- Serve!

Nutrition:

Calories 200, Carbohydrate 30g, Fat 2g, Sugar 6g, Protein 4g, Potassium 350mg, Sodium 100mg, Phosphorus 150mg

Sweet Potato Waffles

Preparation time: 15 mins
Cooking time: 10 mins
Difficulty level: Medium
Serving: 1
PRAL: +1.2

Ingredients:

- 2 cups sweet potatoes, grated
- 2 eggs
- ½ tsp ground cinnamon
- 2 tbsp honey

Instructions:

- Preheat the waffle iron according to the instructions.
- Add honey, ground cinnamon, eggs, & grated sweet potatoes into the mixing bowl & mix well.
- Once the waffle iron is hot, grease with cooking oil.
- Pour the batter into the waffle iron & cook for 5-7 mins.
- Serve!

Nutrition:

Calories 140, Carbohydrate 22g, Fat 4g, Sugar 7g, Protein 4g, Potassium 330mg, Sodium 80mg, Phosphorus 80mg

Oat Pancakes

Preparation time: 5 mins
Cooking time: 5 mins
Difficulty level: Easy
Serving: 1
PRAL: +3.2

Ingredients:

- 1 cup rolled oats
- 2 eggs
- ½ tsp cinnamon

Instructions:

- Add cinnamon, eggs, & oats into the blender & mix & mix.
- Place oil into the intermediate skillet & heat it. Pour batter for pancake & cook for 2-4 mins per side.
- Serve!

Nutrition:

Calories 180, Carbohydrate 33g, Fat 4g, Sugar 9g, Protein 7g, Potassium 390mg, Sodium 85mg, Phosphorus 190mg

APPETIZER RECIPES

Tomato & Cucumber Salad

Preparation time: 5 mins

Cooking time: 0 mins

Difficulty level: Easy

Serving: 1

PRAL: -4.2

Ingredients:

- 2 tomatoes, diced
- 2 cucumbers, diced
- Half red onion, chopped
- 2 tbsp red wine vinegar
- 2 tbsp olive oil

Instructions:

- Add red onion, cucumber, & diced tomatoes into the bowl & mix together.
- Add olive oil, & red wine vinegar in another decent bowl & mix together.
- Pour the dressing over salad & toss well.
- Let it to sit for 10-15 mins.
- Enjoy!

Nutrition:

Calories 100, Carbohydrate 10g, Fat 6g, Sugar 4g, Protein 2g, Potassium 300mg, Sodium 100mg, Phosphorus 40mg

Grilled Eggplant

Preparation time: 10 mins

Cooking time: 5 mins

Difficulty level: Easy

Serving: 1

PRAL: -7.8

Ingredients:

- 1 eggplant
- 2 tbsp olive oil
- 2 cloves garlic, minced
- 2 tbsp fresh parsley, chopped
- 1 tbsp balsamic vinegar

Instructions:

- Firstly, preheat the grill to medium-high heat.
- Rinse & slice the eggplant into rounds.
- Add minced garlic & olive oil into the decent bowl & mix together.
- Apply the eggplant on both sides with olive oil & garlic mixture.
- Put the eggplant onto the grill & saute for 3-4 mins per side.
- Add vinegar & chopped parsley into the bowl & mix well.
- Take out the eggplant from the grill & sprinkle with vinegar mixture.
- Serve!

Nutrition:

Calories 100, Carbohydrate 11g, Fat 7g, Sugar 4g, Protein 1g, Potassium 297mg, Sodium 95mg, Phosphorus 27mg

Baked Zucchini

Preparation time: 10 mins
Cooking time: 25 mins
Difficulty level: Easy
Serving: 1
PRAL: -3.6

Ingredients:

- 4 zucchinis
- Two tbsp olive oil
- 3 cloves garlic, minced
- 1 tsp fresh thyme
- Black pepper, to taste

Instructions:

- Firstly, preheat the oven to 375 degrees F.
- Rinse the zucchini & trim the ends of it. Then, cut into thick slices.
- Add black pepper, thyme, minced garlic, zucchini slices, & olive oil into the medium bowl & toss together.
- Arrange the seasoned zucchini slices onto the baking sheet. Bake for 20-25 mins.
- Take out this from the oven.
- Serve!

Nutrition:

Calories 85, Carbohydrate 7g, Fat 7g, Sugar 3g, Protein 2g, Potassium 360mg, Sodium 290mg, Phosphorus 55mg

Creamed Peas

Preparation time: 10 mins
Cooking time: 10 mins
Difficulty level: Easy
Serving: 1
PRAL: -4.9

Ingredients:

- 2 cups fresh peas
- Half onion, chopped
- ½ cup vegetable broth
- 2-3 fresh mint leaves, chopped
- Black pepper, as desired
- One tbsp butter or olive oil

Instructions:

- Shell & rinse the peas. Add olive oil or butter into the skillet & heat it.
- Place onion & sauté until translucent.
- Add peas & sauté for a few mins. Add vegetable broth & simmer for 5-7 mins.
- Place black pepper, & mint leaves & stir well. Cook for 2-3 mins.
- Serve!

Nutrition:

Calories 90, Carbohydrate 17g, Fat 2g, Sugar 6g, Protein 4g, Potassium 250mg, Sodium 200mg, Phosphorus 90mg

Avocado Stuffing

Preparation time: 15 mins
Cooking time: 0 mins
Difficulty level: Easy
Serving: 1
PRAL: -6.2

Ingredients:

- 2 ripe avocados
- ¼ cup sun-dried tomatoes in oil, drained & chopped
- 1 tbsp capers, drained
- 1 tsp lemon juice
- 2 tbsp olive oil
- ¼ cup black olives, pitted & chopped
- Black pepper, to taste

Instructions:

- Slice the avocado in half and discard the pits.
- Take out the flesh from the avocado.
- Add capers, black olives, & sun-dried tomatoes into the bowl & mix together.
- Add olive oil, lemon zest, & lemon juice to the mixture & sprinkle with black pepper.
- Stuff each avocado half with olive mixture.
- Serve!

Nutrition:

Calories 220, Carbohydrate 12g, Fat 19g, Sugar 2g, Protein 2g, Potassium 570mg, Sodium 260mg, Phosphorus 60mg

Roman-Style Artichokes

Preparation time: 15 mins
Cooking time: 25 mins
Difficulty level: Easy
Serving: 1
PRAL: -3.2

Ingredients:

- 4 artichokes
- 4 cloves of garlic, minced
- ¼ cup fresh parsley, chopped
- 2 tbsp fresh mint, chopped
- ¼ cup olive oil
- 1 tsp lemon juice

Instructions:

- Trim the tough parts of artichoke leaves & cut off the top of each artichoke. Cut in half & remove the choke from the center.
- Add olive oil, mint, parsley, & minced garlic into the bowl & mix together. Add lemon juice & combine together. Brush the artichoke halves with herb mixture.
- Add artichoke into the pot with ½ cup of water & cook for 20-25 mins.
- Apply the herb mixture onto the artichoke.
- Remove them from the pot.
- Serve!

Nutrition:

Calories 200, Carbohydrate 20g, Fat 14g, Sugar 2g, Protein 4g, Potassium 500mg, Sodium 200mg, Phosphorus 100mg

Marinated Peppers

Preparation time: 2-3 hrs
Cooking time: 0 mins
Difficulty level: Easy
Serving: 1
PRAL: -5.1

Ingredients:

- 4 bell peppers
- ¼ cup red wine vinegar
- ¼ cup olive oil
- 2 cloves garlic, minced
- 2 tbsp fresh parsley, chopped

Instructions:

- Rinse & slice the bell peppers into thin strips. Remove the seeds & white membranes.
- Prepare the marinade: Add minced garlic, chopped parsley, olive oil, & red wine vinegar into the mixing bowl & mix well.
- Place the bell pepper strip into the zip-top bag. Add marinade over bell peppers & coat well. Seal the bag & place it into the refrigerator for 2-3 hrs.
- Serve!

Nutrition:

Calories 60, Carbohydrate 4g, Fat 5g, Sugar 2g, Protein 1g, Potassium 140mg, Sodium 80mg, Phosphorus 15mg

Mushrooms Trifoliate

Preparation time: 15 mins
Cooking time: 8 mins
Difficulty level: Easy
Serving: 1
PRAL: -4.7

Ingredients:

- 2 cups button mushrooms
- 2-3 cloves of garlic, minced
- 2 tbsp fresh parsley, chopped
- 2 tbsp olive oil
- 1 tsp lemon juice
- Black pepper, to taste

Instructions:

- Clean the button mushrooms with damp cloth & remove the dirt. Then, cut into small pieces.
- Place olive oil into the decent skillet & heat it. Add minced garlic & sauté for 1 minute.
- Add cleaned mushrooms & cook for 5-7 mins. Season with pepper.
- Once cooked, take out the skillet from the heat.
- Add chopped parsley & lemon juice & mix together.
- Serve!

Nutrition:

Calories 90, Carbohydrate 5g, Fat 7g, Sugar 1g, Protein 2g, Potassium 280mg, Sodium 250mg, Phosphorus 60mg

Hard Boiled Egg

Preparation time: 5 mins
Cooking time: 12 mins
Difficulty level: Easy
Serving: 1
PRAL: +2.1

Ingredients:

- 1 hard-boiled egg
- 1 tbsp mayonnaise
- ½ tsp mustard
- 1 tsp chives, chopped
- 1 pinch black pepper

Instructions:

- Add egg into the medium saucepan & cover it with water & boil & simmer for 9-12 mins.
- Once boiled, cool it in cold water. Then, peel it & cut into half lengthwise.
- Remove the yolk & add it to the bowl. Mash well.
- Add black pepper, chives, mustard, & mayonnaise into the mashed yolk & mix well. Add the filling back into the egg white halves.
- Serve!

Nutrition:

Calories 95, Carbohydrate 0.5g, Fat 8g, Sugar 0.5g, Protein 6g, Potassium 66mg, Sodium 250mg, Phosphorus 96mg

Chickpea Hummus

Preparation time: 15 mins
Cooking time: 0 mins
Difficulty level: Easy
Serving: 1
PRAL: +2.5

Ingredients:

- 1 cup chickpeas, cooked
- 2 tbsp sesame seed oil
- 1-2 cloves garlic
- 1 tsp lemon juice
- 2 tbsp tahini
- ¼ tsp black pepper

Instructions:

- Rinse the cooked chickpeas under cold water & drain them.
- Add black pepper, tahini, lemon juice, & garlic, chickpeas, & sesame seed oil into the blender & mix together.
- Serve!

Nutrition:

Calories 90, Carbohydrate 8g, Fat 5g, Sugar 0g, Protein 3g, Potassium 100mg, Sodium 100mg, Phosphorus 50mg

Seafood First Courses

Whole Wheat Spaghetti with Cherry Tomatoes & Basil

Preparation time: 20 mins
Cooking time: 10 mins
Difficulty level: Easy
Serving: 1
PRAL: -8.3

Ingredients:

- 1 serving of whole wheat spaghetti
- 1 cup fresh cherry tomatoes, halved
- Garlic, 1 to 2 cloves
- ¼ cup basil leaves
- 1 tbsp olive oil
- Pepper, to taste

Instructions:

- Cook the whole wheat spaghetti according to the package instructions until al dente. Drain & set aside.
- Add olive oil into the intermediate skillet & heat it. Place halved cherry tomatoes & cook for 5 mins. Season with pepper. Add basil leaves & cook for 2 mins.
- Add cooked whole wheat spaghetti & toss well.
- Serve!

Nutrition:

Calories 300, Carbohydrate 55g, Fat 7g, Sugar 3g, Protein 10g, Potassium 400mg, Sodium 150mg, Phosphorus 150mg

Risotto with Zucchini & Lemon

Preparation time: 15 mins
Cooking time: 25 mins
Difficulty level: Medium
Serving: 1
PRAL: -4.7

Ingredients:

- Half cup Arborio rice
- 1 zucchini, diced
- 1 tsp lemon zest
- 1 tsp lemon juice
- 2 cups vegetable broth
- Half onion, chopped
- 2 tbsp olive oil

Instructions:

- Add vegetable broth into the saucepan & heat it.
- Place olive oil in another saucepan & heat it. Put onion & sauté it.
- Add Arborio rice & cook for 2 mins.
- Add warm vegetable broth & mix together.
- Cook for 18-20 mins.
- Remove the risotto from the heat.
- Add lemon juice, pepper, & salt & stir well.
- Serve!

Nutrition:

Calories 350, Carbohydrate 61g, Fat 9g, Sugar 2g, Protein 6g, Potassium 250mg, Sodium 600mg, Phosphorus 150mg

Quinoa & Shrimp Salad

Preparation time: 15 mins
Cooking time: 5 mins
Difficulty level: Easy
Serving: 1
PRAL: -1.9

Ingredients:

- ½ cup quinoa
- 6-8 shrimp, peeled & deveined
- ½ avocado, diced
- ½ cucumber, diced
- ½ lemon, juiced
- 2 tbsp parsley, chopped
- Pepper, to taste

Instructions:

- Cook the quinoa according to the package instructions & let it cool.
- Season the shrimp with pepper & salt.
- Place the pan over intermediate heat. Add shrimp & cook for 2-3 mins per side. Remove from heat & allow it to cool.
- Add parsley, cucumber, avocado, shrimp, & quinoa into the mixing bowl & mix well.
- Add lemon juice over the salad & toss together.
- Season with pepper.
- Serve!

Nutrition:

Calories 350, Carbohydrate 30g, Fat 10g, Sugar 1g, Protein 20g, Potassium 500mg, Sodium 250mg, Phosphorus 200mg

Fish Soup with Vegetables

Preparation time: 15 mins
Cooking time: 8 mins
Difficulty level: Easy
Serving: 1
PRAL: -5.6

Ingredients:

- 4 oz mixed fish, such as salmon, cod, & shrimp
- 1 tomatoes, diced
- 1 stalk celery, chopped
- 1 carrot, sliced
- 1 tbsp parsley, chopped

Instructions:

- Add 4 cups of water into the pot & boil it.
- Add mixed fish & simmer for 5 mins. Remove the fish from the pot & keep it aside.
- Add sliced carrots, chopped celery, & diced tomatoes into the same pot & simmer for 10-15 mins.
- Flake the cooked fish into pieces. Add flake fish back to the pot.
- Add chopped parsley & stir well. Simmer for 2-3 mins.
- Season with pepper.
- Serve!

Nutrition:

Calories 160, Carbohydrate 7g, Fat 3g, Sugar 3g, Protein 25g, Potassium 500mg, Sodium 100mg, Phosphorus 200mg

Zucchini Noodles

Preparation time: 15 mins
Cooking time: 0 mins
Difficulty level: Easy
Serving: 1
PRAL: -5.9

Ingredients:

- 1 zucchini
- 1 tsp lemon juice
- 2 tbsp fresh parsley, chopped
- 1 tbsp olive oil

Instructions:

- Trim off the ends of the zucchini with a julienne peeler to create the zucchini noodles.
- Add parsley & zucchini noodles into the bowl & mix well.
- Add lemon juice & olive oil & toss well.
- Serve!

Nutrition:

Calories 160, Carbohydrate 6g, Fat 12g, Sugar 2g, Protein 9g, Potassium 250mg, Sodium 100mg, Phosphorus 150mg

Couscous with Calamari & Vegetables

Preparation time: 15 mins
Cooking time: 15-20 mins
Difficulty level: Easy
Serving: 1
PRAL: -3.8

Ingredients:

- ½ cup whole wheat couscous
- 4 oz calamari, cleaned & sliced into rings
- 1 zucchini, diced
- Half bell pepper, diced
- Half onion, chopped
- 2 tbsp olive oil
- Pepper, to taste

Instructions:

- Add water into the pot & boil it. Add couscous & cover, allow it sit for 5 mins. Then, fluff with a fork.
- Add 1 tbsp of olive oil into the pan & boil it. Add calamari & cook for 2-3 mins.
- Remove from the pan. Keep it aside.
- Add remaining 1 tbsp of olive oil in another pan & heat it. Add onion & sauté it.
- Add bell pepper & zucchini & sauté for 5-7 mins.
- Add cooked calamari to the pan & season with pepper. Cook for 2-3 mins.
- Serve calamari mixture over couscous.
- Serve!

Nutrition:

Calories 350, Carbohydrate 45g, Fat 12g, Sugar 3g, Protein 15g, Potassium 400mg, Sodium 300mg, Phosphorus 200mg

Seafood Salad with Avocado

Preparation time: 10 mins
Cooking time: 0 mins
Difficulty level: Easy
Serving: 1
PRAL: -2.2

Ingredients:

- 3 oz mixed seafood, mussels, clams, shrimp, sautéed or steamed
- Half avocado
- 1 tsp lemon juice
- 1 tbsp parsley, chopped

Instructions:

- Cut the avocado in half, remove the pit & scoop out the flesh. Then, cut into small pieces. Add lemon juice over diced avocado.
- Add mixed & sautéed seafood & avocado into the bowl & toss well. Add chopped parsley & toss together.
- Enjoy!

Nutrition:

Calories 200, Carbohydrate 9g, Fat 13g, Sugar 1g, Protein 13g, Potassium 450mg, Sodium 300mg, Phosphorus 200mg

Chickpea Pasta with Shrimp

Preparation time: 10 mins
Cooking time: 15 mins
Difficulty level: Easy
Serving: 1
PRAL: -4.1

Ingredients:

- 1 cup chickpea pasta
- 8-10 shrimp, peeled & deveined
- ¼ cup dried cherry tomatoes
- 2 cloves garlic, minced
- 1 red chili pepper, chopped
- 2 tbsp olive oil
- Pepper, To Taste

Instructions:

- Add water into the pot & boil it. Add chickpea pasta & cook for 7-9 mins. Drain & keep it aside.
- Add olive oil into the skillet & heat it. Add chopped chili & garlic & sauté for 1-2 mins.
- Place peeled & deveined shrimp & cook for 2-3 mins per side.
- Season with pepper. Add cooked chickpea pasta & cherry tomatoes & toss well. Cook for 1-2 mins.
- Enjoy!

Nutrition:

Calories 350, Carbohydrate 40-45g, Fat 12g, Sugar 3g, Protein 20g, Potassium 400mg, Sodium 250mg, Phosphorus 250mg

Black Risotto with Squid & Peas

Preparation time: 20 mins
Cooking time: 40-45 mins
Difficulty level: Easy
Serving: 1
PRAL: +0.3

Ingredients:

- ½ cup black rice
- ¼ cup sliced calamari
- ¼ cup peas
- 1 cup vegetable broth
- 1/4 onion, chopped
- 1 tbsp olive oil

Instructions:

- Rinse the black rice under cold water & drain it.
- Add olive oil into the saucepan & heat it. Add chopped onion & sauté for 2-3 mins.
- Add black rice & sauté for 2-3 mins. Add vegetable broth & boil it. Simmer for 30-35 mins until tender.
- Place the pan over intermediate heat. Add sliced calamari & cook for 2-3 mins. Keep it aside.
- Add peas into the rice & stir well. Add cooked calamari to the rice mixture & cook for 2 mins.
- Enjoy!

Nutrition:

Calories 350, Carbohydrate 50g, Fat 10g, Sugar 3g, Protein 15g, Potassium 300mg, Sodium 500mg, Phosphorus 150mg

Zucchini Spaghetti with Anchovy Sauce

Preparation time: 5 mins
Cooking time: 10 mins
Difficulty level: Easy
Serving: 1
PRAL: +1.6

Ingredients:

- 1 zucchini
- 2-3 anchovy fillets in oil
- 1 clove of garlic, minced
- ¼ tsp red chili flakes
- 2 tbsp olive oil
- Pepper, to taste

Instructions:

- Spiralize the zucchini with a spiralizer to create a zucchini noodles. Keep it aside.
- Add olive oil into the pot. Add red chili flakes & garlic & sauté for 1 minute. Add anchovy fillets & cook for 2-3 mins. Add zucchini spaghetti & cook for 2-3 mins. Season with pepper.
- Enjoy!

Nutrition:

Calories 150, Carbohydrate 4g, Fat 13g, Sugar 2g, Protein 4g, Potassium 350mg, Sodium 500mg, Phosphorus 70mg

Land First Courses

Lentil & Tomato Soup

Preparation time: 15 mins
Cooking time: 30 mins
Difficulty level: Easy
Serving: 1
PRAL: -2.4

Ingredients:

- ¼ cup dried lentils
- ½ cup tomatoes, diced
- ¼ cup onion, diced
- ¼ cup celery, diced
- ¼ cup carrots, diced
- 1 tbsp parsley, chopped
- 1 cup vegetable broth, low-sodium
- Pepper, to taste

Instructions:

- Rinse the lentils under cold water & then drain it.
- Add water or vegetable broth into the saucepan & boil it.
- Add carrot, celery, & onion to the saucepan & cook for 5 mins.
- Add parsley, tomatoes, & lentils & mix together. Add vegetable broth & simmer for 20-25 mins. Season with pepper & salt.
- Enjoy!

Nutrition:

Calories 200, Carbohydrate 40g, Fat 1g, Sugar 6g, Protein 10g, Potassium 400mg, Sodium 200mg, Phosphorus 200mg

Zucchini Spaghetti with Avocado Pesto

Preparation time: 15 mins
Cooking time: 0 mins
Difficulty level: Easy
Serving: 1
PRAL: -2.1

Ingredients:

- 1 zucchini
- Half ripe avocado
- ¼ cup fresh basil leaves
- 1 tbsp olive oil
- 2 tbsp walnuts
- 1 garlic clove
- Pepper, to taste

Instructions:

- Spiralize the zucchini with a spiralizer to create a zucchini noodles. Keep it aside.
- Add garlic, walnuts, olive oil, basil, & avocado into the blender & mix and mix. Season with pepper.
- Add zucchini spaghetti & avocado pesto into the bowl & mix together.
- Enjoy!

Nutrition:

Calories 320, Carbohydrate 14g, Fat 28g, Sugar 2g, Protein 6g, Potassium 660mg, Sodium 150mg, Phosphorus 120mg

Quinoa with Grilled Vegetables

Preparation time: 10 mins
Cooking time: 20 mins
Difficulty level: Easy
Serving: 1
PRAL: -1.7

Ingredients:

- ½ cup quinoa
- ½ zucchini, sliced
- Half bell pepper, sliced
- Half eggplant, sliced
- 1 tbsp olive oil
- ½ tsp dried oregano
- Pepper, to taste

Instructions:

- Rinse the quinoa under cold water to remove any bitterness. Drain well.
- Add 1 cup of water & quinoa into the saucepan & boil & simmer for 15 mins. Remove from heat & allow it to sit for 5 mins. Fluff with a fork.
- Preheat the grill over medium-high heat.
- Add pepper, oregano, olive oil, eggplant, bell pepper, & sliced zucchini into the bowl & mix well.
- Grill for 3-4 mins per side.
- Add over cooked quinoa.
- Enjoy!

Nutrition:

Calories 300, Carbohydrate 45g, Fat 10g, Sugar 5g, Protein 8g, Potassium 470mg, Sodium 20mg, Phosphorus 120mg

Spinach & Strawberry Salad

Preparation time: 10 mins
Cooking time: 0 mins
Difficulty level: Easy
Serving: 1
PRAL: -3.5

Ingredients:

- 2 cups fresh spinach leaves
- 1 cup sliced strawberries
- 2 tbsp slivered almonds
- ¼ cup crumbled feta cheese, crumbled
- 1 tbsp balsamic vinegar

Instructions:

- Rinse & dry the spinach leaves.
- Cut the strawberries & keep it side.
- Add slivered almonds into the skillet & sauté until browned.
- Add crumbled feta cheese, almonds, strawberries, & spinach into the salad bowl & mix well. Add balsamic vinegar & toss well.
- Enjoy!

Nutrition:

Calories 250, Carbohydrate 15g, Fat 17g, Sugar 8g, Protein 9g, Potassium 400mg, Sodium 350mg, Phosphorus 200mg

Couscous with Vegetables & Cucumbers

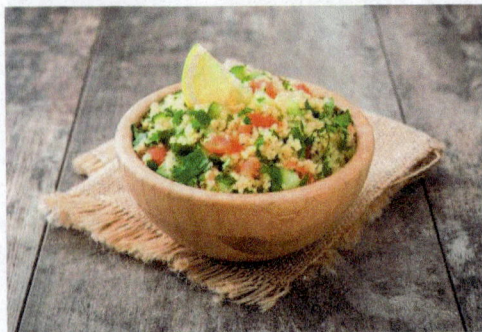

Preparation time: 10 mins
Cooking time: 5 mins
Difficulty level: Easy
Serving: 1
PRAL: -1.9

Ingredients:

- ½ cup couscous
- 1 tomato, diced
- Half cucumber, diced
- 2 tbsp mint leaves, chopped
- 2 tbsp parsley, chopped
- One tsp lemon juice
- Pepper, to taste

Instructions:

- Add ½ cup of water into the intermediate pot & boil it. Add boiling water over the couscous into the bowl & cover with a lid. Let it sit for 5 mins. Fluff with a fork.
- Add chopped parsley, mint, & cucumber, diced tomatoes, & cooked couscous into the mixing bowl & mix well.
- Add lemon juice & pepper & toss well.
- Enjoy!

Nutrition:

Calories 250, Carbohydrate 50g, Fat 1g, Sugar 3g, Protein 8g, Potassium 300mg, Sodium 150mg, Phosphorus 120mg

Risotto with Zucchini & Lemon

Preparation time: 15 mins
Cooking time: 25-30 mins
Difficulty level: Easy
Serving: 1
PRAL: -2.0

Ingredients:

- ½ cup Arborio rice
- 1 zucchini, diced
- 1 tsp lemon juice
- 1 tsp lemon zest
- 1 ½ cups vegetable broth
- 2 tbsp cheese, grated
- Black pepper, to taste

Instructions:

- Pour vegetable broth into the saucepan & boil it.
- Add olive oil in another saucepan & boil it. Add diced zucchini & sauté for 4-5 mins. Keep it aside.
- Add Arborio rice into the same saucepan & toast for 1-2 mins.
- Add vegetable broth & cook for 15 to 18 mins.
- Add lemon juice, lemon zest, & cooked zucchini & cook for 2-3 mins.
- Remove the pan from the flame.
- Enjoy!

Nutrition:

Calories 350, Carbohydrate 60g, Fat 8g, Sugar 3g, Protein 9g, Potassium 300mg, Sodium 800mg, Phosphorus 180mg

Whole-Wheat Pasta with Sun-Dried Tomatoes & Capers

Preparation time: 5 mins
Cooking time: 10 mins
Difficulty level: Easy
Serving: 1
PRAL: -1.8

Ingredients:

- 1 cup of whole-wheat pasta
- 2-3 sun-dried tomatoes, chopped
- 1 tbsp capers
- 1 clove garlic, minced
- 1 tbsp fresh parsley, chopped
- 1 tbsp olive oil
- Pepper, to taste

Instructions:

- Cook the whole-wheat pasta in a pot of boiling salted water according to the package instructions until al dente. Drain & set aside.
- Add capers & sun-dried tomatoes into the saucepan & cook for 2-3 mins. Season with pepper. Add cooked pasta & toss well.
- Take out the pan from the heat.
- Enjoy!

Nutrition:

Calories 350, Carbohydrate 70g, Fat 3g, Sugar 2g, Protein 10g, Potassium 400mg, Sodium 600mg, Phosphorus 200mg

Carrot Casserole

Preparation time: 15 mins
Cooking time: 40 mins
Difficulty level: Easy
Serving: 1
PRAL: -1.3

Ingredients:

- 2 cups carrots, sliced
- 2 eggs
- ½ cup cheese, grated
- ½ cup milk
- Pepper, to taste

Instructions:

- Firstly, preheat the oven to 350 degrees F.
- Add water into the saucepan & boil it. Add carrots & cook for 5 to 7 mins. Drain & keep them aside.
- Add eggs into the bowl & beat together. Add pepper, milk, & grated cheese & mix it.
- Layer the cooked carrots into the casserole dish. Add egg & cheese mixture over veggies. Bake for 25 to 30 mins.
- Enjoy!

Nutrition:

Calories 230, Carbohydrate 18g, Fat 14g, Sugar 4g, Protein 11g, Potassium 570mg, Sodium 280mg, Phosphorus 250mg

Baked Ratatouille

Preparation time: 15 mins
Cooking time: 35 mins
Difficulty level: Easy
Serving: 1
PRAL: 2.0

Ingredients:

- Half eggplant, diced
- Half zucchini, diced
- Half bell pepper, diced
- 1 tomato, diced
- 1 clove garlic, minced
- 1 tbsp olive oil
- Pepper to taste

Instructions:

- Firstly, preheat the oven to 375 degrees F.
- Add garlic, tomato, bell pepper, zucchini, & eggplant into the baking dish & mix well. Add olive oil & pepper & toss well.
- Cover the dish with foil. Bake for 30-35 mins.
- Enjoy!

Nutrition:

Calories 150, Carbohydrate 15g, Fat 10g, Sugar 7g, Protein 2g, Potassium 500mg, Sodium 250mg, Phosphorus 50mg

Herb Risotto

Preparation time: 15 mins
Cooking time: 20 mins
Difficulty level: Easy
Serving: 1
PRAL: 2.1

Ingredients:

- Half cup Arborio rice
- 1 tbsp fresh parsley, chopped
- 1 tbsp fresh basil, chopped
- 1 tbsp fresh mint, chopped
- 1 ½ cups vegetable broth, low-sodium
- 2 tbsp cheese, grated

Instructions:

- Add vegetable broth into the saucepan & boil it. Reduce the heat to low.
- Add Arborio rice into the saucepan & heat it for 1-2 mins.
- Add vegetable broth & simmer for 18-20 mins. Then, add chopped parsley, mint, & basil & stir well.
- Once rice is cooked, take out it from the heat.
- Add grated cheese & mix together.
- Enjoy!

Nutrition:

Calories 300, Carbohydrate 50g, Fat 6g, Sugar 1g, Protein 8g, Potassium 300mg, Sodium 200mg, Phosphorus 200mg

Seafood Main Courses

Grilled Lemon Salmon

Preparation time: 10 mins
Cooking time: 7-9 mins
Difficulty level: Easy
Serving: 1
PRAL: -8.5

Ingredients:

- 4-6 oz salmon fillet
- 1 tbsp lemon juice
- 1 tbsp olive oil
- ¼ tsp black pepper

Instructions:

- Preheat the grill to medium-high heat.
- Add olive oil & lemon juice into the decent bowl & mix well. Apply the mixture over salmon fillets & season with black pepper. Place it onto the grill & cook for 3-4 mins per side.
- Remove the salmon from the grill & let it sit for a minute.
- Enjoy!

Nutrition:

Calories 250, Carbohydrate 2g, Fat 15g, Sugar 0.5g, Protein 26g, Potassium 450mg, Sodium 250mg, Phosphorus 300mg

Fresh Tuna Tartare

Preparation time: 30 mins
Cooking time: 0 mins
Difficulty level: Easy
Serving: 1
PRAL: -5.6

Ingredients:

- 3.5 oz fresh tuna, diced
- ¼ red onion, chopped
- ¼ cucumber, diced
- 1 tsp lime juice
- Pepper, to taste

Instructions:

- Add cucumber & red onion into the bowl & mix together.
- Add lime juice & stir well. Season with pepper. Place it into the fridge for 15 to 30 mins.
- Enjoy!

Nutrition:

Calories 160, Carbohydrate 5g, Fat 5g, Sugar 2g, Protein 25g, Potassium 300mg, Sodium 200mg, Phosphorus 200mg

Salmon & Shrimp Skewers

Preparation time: 5 mins
Cooking time: 10 mins
Difficulty level: Easy
Serving: 1
PRAL: -5.7

Ingredients:

- 3-4 oz salmon cubes
- 3-4 shrimp, peeled & deveined
- Half bell pepper, sliced
- ¼ onion, sliced

Instructions:

- Preheat your grill or broiler to medium-high heat.
- Thread the salmon cubes, bell pepper, shrimp, & onion onto the skewers. Brush with olive oil & season with lemon zest, garlic powder, pepper, & salt.
- Place onto the grill & cook for 3-4 mins per side.
- Enjoy!

Nutrition:

Calories 250, Carbohydrate 7g, Fat 10g, Sugar 2g, Protein 30g, Potassium 500mg, Sodium 300mg, Phosphorus 300mg

Cartoccio Trout with Aromatic Herbs

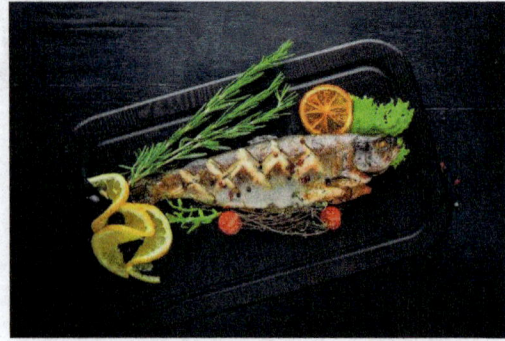

Preparation time: 15 mins
Cooking time: 20 mins
Difficulty level: Medium
Serving: 1
PRAL: -7.8

Ingredients:

- 4-6 oz trout fillet
- Fresh aromatic herbs, thyme, rosemary, parsley
- Half lemon, thinly sliced
- Pepper, to taste

Instructions:

- Firstly, preheat your oven to 375 degrees F.
- Place the trout fillet in the middle of the parchment paper.
- Season the trout fillets with pepper.
- Place aromatic herb & lemon slices over trout fillet.
- Fold the parchment paper over the trout to create a packet. Seal it. Place onto the baking sheet & bake for 15 to 20 mins.
- Enjoy!

Nutrition:

Calories 200, Carbohydrate 2g, Fat 6g, Sugar 0.5g, Protein 20g, Potassium 350mg, Sodium 250mg, Phosphorus 200mg

Sole with Lemon & Capers

Preparation time: 10 mins
Cooking time: 5 mins
Difficulty level: Easy
Serving: 1
PRAL: -5.2

Ingredients:

- 4-6 oz sole fillet
- 1 tsp lemon juice
- 1 tbsp capers
- 1 tbsp butter
- Pepper, to taste

Instructions:

- Season the sole fillet with pepper.
- Add butter into the intermediate skillet & heat it. Add sole fillets & cook for 2-3 mins per side.
- Add capers & cook for 1-2 mins. Add lemon juice over sole & capers & cook for 1 minute.
- Enjoy!

Nutrition:

Calories 200, Carbohydrate 3g, Fat 15g, Sugar 1g, Protein 25g, Potassium 300mg, Sodium 100mg, Phosphorus 200mg

Grilled Swordfish

Preparation time: 10 mins
Cooking time: 10 mins
Difficulty level: Easy
Serving: 1
PRAL: -8.3

Ingredients:

- 6-8 oz swordfish fillet
- 1 tbsp olive oil
- Black pepper, to taste

Instructions:

- Firstly, preheat your grill to medium-high heat.
- Apply the swordfish fillet with olive oil. Season with pepper & salt.
- Place the swordfish fillets onto the grill grates. Grill for 4-5 mins per side.
- Enjoy!

Nutrition:

Calories 250, Carbohydrate 0g, Fat 15g, Sugar 0g, Protein 25g, Potassium 450mg, Sodium 50mg, Phosphorus 250mg

Baked Crab Meatballs

Preparation time: 10 mins
Cooking time: 20 mins
Difficulty level: Easy
Serving: 1
PRAL: -4.1

Ingredients:

- 8 oz crab meat
- ½ cup bread crumbs, without salt
- 1 egg
- 1 tbsp mixed herbs
- Pepper, to taste

Instructions:

- Firstly, preheat your oven to 375 degrees F.
- Add mixed herbs, egg, breadcrumbs, & crab meat into the mixing bowl & mix well.
- Add pepper & mix well.
- Shape the mixture into meatballs & place them onto the baking sheet lined with parchment paper. Bake for 15 to 20 mins.
- Remove from the oven.
- Enjoy!

Nutrition:

Calories 150, Carbohydrate 12g, Fat 6g, Sugar 1g, Protein 12g, Potassium 200mg, Sodium 100mg, Phosphorus 150mg

Shrimp Tempura

Preparation time: 10 mins
Cooking time: 10 mins
Difficulty level: Easy
Serving: 1
PRAL: +4.2

Ingredients:

- 6 shrimp, peeled & deveined
- ½ cup rice flour
- 1 egg
- Olive oil, for frying

Instructions:

- Put olive oil into the pan.
- Place egg into the bowl & beat well. Add rice flour in another bowl. Dip each shrimp into the beaten egg & coat it. Then, roll it into the rice flour. Add coated shrimp into the hot oil & fry it.
- Remove the shrimp from the oil.
- Enjoy!

Nutrition:

Calories 180, Carbohydrate 25g, Fat 7g, Sugar 0g, Protein 10g, Potassium 100mg, Sodium 100mg, Phosphorus 80mg

Fish Soup with Garlic Croutons

Preparation time: 15 mins
Cooking time: 20 mins
Difficulty level: Easy
Serving: 1
PRAL: +2.8

Ingredients:

- 4 oz fish
- 2 tomatoes, diced
- 2 cloves garlic, minced
- 2 slices of whole wheat bread
- 1 tbsp olive oil
- Pepper, to taste

Instructions:

- Add olive oil into the pan & heat it. Add garlic & sauté for 1-2 mins.
- Add diced tomatoes & cook for 5 mins. Add 2 cups of water & simmer for 10 mins.
- Prepare the garlic croutons: Toast the whole wheat bread until crispy. Rub with garlic. Season with pepper.
- Add fish soup into the bowl & top with garlic croutons.
- Enjoy!

Nutrition:

Calories 300, Carbohydrate 20g, Fat 10g, Sugar 3g, Protein 25g, Potassium 200mg, Sodium 100mg, Phosphorus 80mg

Tuna Patties

Preparation time: 10 mins
Cooking time: 10 mins
Difficult level: Easy
Serving: 12
PRAL: - 4.2

Ingredients:

- Tuna, 15 oz
- Salt, ½ tsp
- Pepper, ½ tsp
- Curry powder, 1 tbsp
- Breadcrumbs, 1 cup
- Eggs, 2, beaten
- Mayonnaise, 3 tbsp
- Worcestershire sauce, 1 tsp
- Parsley, ¼ cup, chopped

Instructions:

- Add curry powder, pepper, salt, garlic, & tuna to the mixing bowl & combine well.
- Add remaining ingredients & stir until smooth.
- Shape the mixture into the patties.
- Add oil into the medium pan & heat it. Add patties & fry until crispy.
- Serve!

Nutrition:

Calories 58kcal, Carbohydrate 2g, Protein 6g, Fat 2g, Fiber 1g

Land Main Courses

Turkey Taco with Avocado Sauce

Preparation time: 10 mins
Cooking time: 10 mins
Difficulty level: Medium
Serving: 1
PRAL: -3.1

Ingredients:

- 4 oz ground turkey meat
- Half avocado
- 1 tomato
- 1 cup lettuce, shredded
- Pepper to taste

Instructions:

- Place ground turkey meat into the decent skillet & cook it. Add pepper & sauté for 5 to 7 mins.
- Prepare the avocado sauce: Add avocado flesh & salt into the bowl & mix well.
- Assemble: Lay the lettuce leaf, add cooked turkey meat, diced tomato, & dollop of avocado over it.
- Serve!

Nutrition:

Calories 230, Carbohydrate 9g, Fat 15g, Sugar 2g, Protein 17g, Potassium 200mg, Sodium 100mg, Phosphorus 150mg

Eggplant Cutlet with Mixed Salad

Preparation time: 10 mins
Cooking time: 5-8 mins
Difficulty level: Medium
Serving: 1
PRAL: -3.5

Ingredients:

- 1 eggplant
- 1 egg
- ½ cup all-purpose flour
- Lettuce leaves
- 1 tomato
- Olive oil for frying
- Pepper to taste

Instructions:

- Wash & peel the eggplant. Slice into rounds.
- Sprinkle with black pepper & allow it sit for 10 mins. After 10 mins, rinse the eggplant slices under cold water. Then, pat it dry with a paper towel.
- Add egg into the bowl & beat well. Add flour in another bowl.
- Add olive oil into the pot & heat it. Dip each eggplant slice in beaten egg & then in flour. Place the coated eggplant slices into the oil & fry for 2-3 mins per side.
- Prepare the mixed salad: Rinse & tear the lettuce leaves into pieces.
- Dice the tomato into pieces.
- Serve with eggplant.

Nutrition:

Calories 250, Carbohydrate 29g, Fat 13g, Sugar 3g, Protein 6g, Potassium 300mg, Sodium 250mg, Phosphorus 120mg

Duck Breast with Blueberries & Spinach

Preparation time: 10 mins
Cooking time: 25 mins
Difficulty level: Medium
Serving: 1
PRAL: -2.8

Ingredients:

- 1 duck breast
- 1 cup fresh blueberries
- 2 cups fresh spinach
- Pepper to taste

Instructions:

- Firstly, preheat the oven to 400 degrees F.
- Season the duck breast with pepper.
- Add duck breast into the skillet & cook for 4-5 mins. Flip & cook for 2 mins.
- Transfer the skillet of duck breast into the oven & roast for 8 to 10 mins.
- Add spinach into the separate pan & sauté for 2 mins.
- Remove the duck breast from the oven.
- Serve!

Nutrition:

Calories 300, Carbohydrate 8g, Fat 18g, Sugar 4g, Protein 30g, Potassium 450mg, Sodium 200mg, Phosphorus 250mg

Vegan Sausages with Peperonata

Preparation time: 10 mins
Cooking time: 15 mins
Difficulty level: Easy
Serving: 1
PRAL: -3.0

Ingredients:

- 2 vegan sausages
- 2 bell peppers
- 1 onion
- 1 tbsp olive oil
- Pepper to taste

Instructions:

- Add olive oil into the pot & heat it. Add sliced peppers & onion & sauté for 10-15 mins until tender.
- Prepare the vegan sausage according the packet instructions.
- Add pepper into the pot & stir well.
- Place the vegan sausages onto the plate. Top with pepperonata.
- Enjoy!

Nutrition:

Calories 300, Carbohydrate 15g, Fat 10g, Sugar 5g, Protein 15g, Potassium 150mg, Sodium 200mg, Phosphorus 150mg

Quinoa & Black Bean Burgers

Preparation time: 10 mins
Cooking time: 10 mins
Difficulty level: Easy
Serving: 1
PRAL: -1.9

Ingredients:

- ½ cup quinoa
- 1 cup black beans, cooked & drained
- ¼ cup onion, chopped
- ¼ cup bell pepper, chopped
- 1 tsp black pepper

Instructions:

- Cook the quinoa according to the package instructions & let it cool.
- Add black pepper, bell pepper, onion, black beans, & cooked quinoa into the blender & mix & mix. Shape the mixture into patties.
- Add small amount of olive oil into the pan & heat it. Add patties & fry for 4-5 mins per side.
- Enjoy!

Nutrition:

Calories 180, Carbohydrate 35g, Fat 2g, Sugar 2g, Protein 8g, Potassium 90mg, Sodium 150mg, Phosphorus 100mg

Roast Pork with Apple Sauce

Preparation time: 10 mins
Cooking time: 30 mins
Difficulty level: Easy
Serving: 1
PRAL: -3.3

Ingredients:

- 4 oz pork tenderloin
- 1 apple
- ¼ tsp cinnamon
- Pepper, to taste

Instructions:

- Preheat the oven to 375 degrees F.
- Season the pork tenderloin with pepper & cinnamon.
- Place the pork onto the baking sheet. Bake for 25-30 mins.
- Prepare the apple sauce: Peel, core, & chop the apple into small pieces.
- Add chopped apple, cinnamon, & 2-3 tbsp of water into the cooking pan & simmer over low heat. Stir until mashed.
- Serve with sauce.

Nutrition:

Calories 230, Carbohydrate 20g, Fat 4g, Sugar 15g, Protein 25g, Potassium 250mg, Sodium 100mg, Phosphorus 200mg

Cabbage Rolls with Wild Rice

Preparation time: 15 mins
Cooking time: 5 mins
Difficulty level: Easy
Serving: 1
PRAL: -2.5

Ingredients:

- 4-6 cabbage leaves
- 1 cup wild rice, cooked
- 1 cup mushrooms, chopped
- Pepper to taste
- Olive oil for sautéing

Instructions:

- Add water into the pot & boil it. Add cabbage leaves & boil for 2-3 mins. Then, remove & keep it aside.
- Prepare the filling: Add olive oil into the pot. Add chopped mushrooms & sauté it. Season with black pepper.
- Add cooked rice & sautéed mushroom into the bowl & mix well.
- Lay a cabbage leaf; place a mushroom mixture at the center. Fold the sides of the cabbage leaf over the filling & roll it up.
- Serve!

Nutrition:

Calories 200, Carbohydrate 40g, Fat 3g, Sugar 2g, Protein 5g, Potassium 100mg, Sodium 100mg, Phosphorus 100mg

Beef Steak with Balsamic & Mushroom Reduction

Preparation time: 15 mins
Cooking time: 10 mins
Difficulty level: Medium
Serving: 1
PRAL: 4.1

Ingredients:

- 4-6 oz beef steak
- 1 cup mushrooms, sliced
- 2 tbsp balsamic vinegar
- Pepper to taste
- 1-2 tsp olive oil

Instructions:

- Season the steak with pepper.
- Add 1-2 tsp of olive oil into the intermediate skillet. Place seasoned steaks & cook for 3-5 mins per side. Remove the steak from the skillet.
- Prepare the reduction: Add sliced mushroom into the same pan & cook for 5-7 mins. Place balsamic vinegar & stir well.
- Cut the steaks into strips. Add reduction over it.
- Serve!

Nutrition:

Calories 250, Carbohydrate 5g, Fat 10g, Sugar 2g, Protein 30g, Potassium 400mg, Sodium 150mg, Phosphorus 250mg

Honey Glazed Pork Ribs

Preparation time: 15 mins
Cooking time: 2 hours
Difficulty level: Medium
Serving: 1
PRAL: 5.2

Ingredients:

- 1 lb pork ribs
- ¼ cup honey
- 2 tbsp mustard
- Pepper to taste

Instructions:

- Preheat the oven to 325 degrees F.
- Add mustard & honey into the bowl & mix well.
- Sprinkle the pork rib with pepper.
- Place the pork rib onto the baking sheet lined with foil. Brush the glaze over pork ribs.
- Bake for 2 hours.
- Serve!

Nutrition:

Calories 650, Carbohydrate 20g, Fat 45g, Sugar 18g, Protein 40g, Potassium 500mg, Sodium 300mg, Phosphorus 350mg

Rosemary Chicken with a side of Asparagus

Preparation time: 15 mins
Cooking time: 25 mins
Difficulty level: Easy
Serving: 1
PRAL: -3.2

Ingredients:

- 1 boneless, skinless chicken breast
- 1 tbsp fresh rosemary leaves
- 8-10 fresh asparagus spears
- Pepper to taste
- Olive oil, for cooking

Instructions:

- Preheat your oven to 375 degrees F.
- Season the chicken breasts with pepper.
- Add olive oil into the intermediate skillet & heat it. Place chicken breast & sear for 2-3 mins per side.
- Transfer the seared chicken breast into the dish. Add asparagus around it. Add olive oil & pepper. Bake for 15 to 20 mins.
- Enjoy it.

Nutrition:

Calories 250, Carbohydrate 6g, Fat 8g, Sugar 2g, Protein 40g, Potassium 550mg, Sodium 200mg, Phosphorus 350mg

Soups

Tomato & Basil Soup

Preparation time: 10 mins
Cooking time: 15 mins
Difficulty level: Easy
Serving: 1
PRAL: -3.5

Ingredients:

- 1 cup fresh tomatoes, diced
- ¼ cup fresh basil leaves, chopped
- ¼ cup onion, chopped
- 1 clove garlic, minced
- 1 cup vegetable broth, low-sodium

Instructions:

- Place olive oil into the saucepan & heat it. Add onion & garlic & sauté it.
- Add basil & tomatoes & cook for 5 mins. Add vegetable broth & simmer for 10-15 mins.
- Transfer the mixture to the blender & mix & mix.
- Return the mixture to the saucepan & heat it. Season with pepper.
- Serve!

Nutrition:

Calories 100, Carbohydrate 20g, Fat 2g, Sugar 10g, Protein 3g, Potassium 250mg, Sodium 100mg, Phosphorus 40mg

Vegetable Minestrone

Preparation time: 10 mins
Cooking time: 20 mins
Difficulty level: Easy
Serving: 1
PRAL: -5.2

Ingredients:

- 1 zucchini, sliced
- 1 cup green beans, trimmed & chopped
- 2 carrots, diced
- 2 tomatoes, diced
- 1 onion, chopped
- 2 celery stalks, diced
- 4 cups vegetable broth, low-sodium
- Pepper, to taste

Instructions:

- Add oil into the pot & heat it. Add onion & sauté for a few mins.
- Add green beans, carrots, & celery & sauté for 5 mins. Add vegetable broth & simmer it. Reduce the heat, add tomatoes & zucchini & stir well.
- Simmer for 15 to 20 mins until tender. Season with pepper.
- Serve!

Nutrition:

Calories 80, Carbohydrate 17g, Fat 0.5g, Sugar 6g, Protein 2g, Potassium 500mg, Sodium 140mg, Phosphorus 40mg

Lentil Soup

Preparation time: 15 mins
Cooking time: 40 mins
Difficulty level: Easy
Serving: 1
PRAL: -4.7

Ingredients:

- 1 cup dried lentils, rinsed & drained
- 1 onion, chopped
- 2 stalks of celery
- 1 bay leaf
- 2 carrots, peeled & chopped
- 4 cups vegetable, low-sodium
- One to two cloves garlic
- 1 tsp olive oil
- Pepper to taste

Instructions:

- Add olive oil into the pot & heat it. Add carrots, celery, & chopped onion & cook for 5-7 mins. Add minced garlic & sauté for 1 minute. Add bay leaf & rinsed lentils to the pot. Then, add broth & boil it.
- Lower the heat & cover the pot. Cook for 25 to 30 mins.
- Season with pepper.
- Discard bay leaf.
- Serve!

Nutrition:

Calories 200, Carbohydrate 40g, Fat 1g, Sugar 5g, Protein 13g, Potassium 500mg, Sodium 240mg, Phosphorus 250mg

Cream of Pumpkin Soup

Preparation time: 15 mins

Cooking time: 35 mins

Difficulty level: Easy

Serving: 1

PRAL: -2.8

Ingredients:

- 1 cup pumpkin, diced
- ½ cup onion, chopped
- 2 cups vegetable or chicken broth, low-sodium
- ¼ tsp nutmeg
- Pepper to taste
- 1 tbsp olive oil

Instructions:

- Add olive oil into the pot & heat it. Add chopped onion & sauté for 3-5 mins. Then, add nutmeg & pumpkin & sauté for 2-3 mins. Add broth & boil it. Reduce the heat & simmer for 20-25 mins.
- Transfer the mixture to the blender & blend until smooth.
- Season with pepper.
- Enjoy!

Nutrition:

Calories 100, Carbohydrate 20g, Fat 2g, Sugar 5g, Protein 2g, Potassium 500mg, Sodium 200mg, Phosphorus 60mg

Chicken & Rice Soup

Preparation time: 15 mins
Cooking time: 50 mins
Difficulty level: Easy
Serving: 1
PRAL: -2.0

Ingredients:

- 4 oz chicken breast, boneless, skinless
- ¼ cup white rice, low-sodium
- ¼ cup carrots, diced
- ¼ cup celery, diced
- 1 cup chicken broth, low-sodium

Instructions:

- Poach the chicken breast in water for 15-20 mins until cooked. Then, shred the chicken into pieces.
- Add white rice & chicken broth into the pot & simmer & cook for 15-20 mins.
- Add celery & diced carrots & cook for 5 to 10 mins.
- Add shredded chicken & cook for few mins.
- Season with pepper.
- Serve!

Nutrition:

Calories 250, Carbohydrate 18g, Fat 3g, Sugar 5g, Protein 2g, Potassium 300mg, Sodium 200mg, Phosphorus 200mg

Spinach Soup

Preparation time: 15 mins
Cooking time: 30 mins
Difficulty level: Easy
Serving: 1
PRAL: -3.9

Ingredients:

- 1 cup fresh spinach, washed & chopped
- 1 onion, chopped
- 2 cups vegetable broth, low-sodium
- Pepper to taste

Instructions:

- Add a splash of water or cooking spray into the intermediate pot. Add onion & cook for 3-5 mins. Pour vegetable broth & simmer it.
- Reduce the heat & cover the pot. Simmer for 15 to 20 mins.
- Then, add spinach & cook for 2-3 mins.
- Add the mixture into the blender & mix & mix.
- Place the mixture back to the pot & heat it.
- Season with pepper.
- Serve!

Nutrition:

Calories 120, Carbohydrate 26g, Fat 0.5g, Sugar 2g, Protein 3g, Potassium 800mg, Sodium 150mg, Phosphorus 70mg

Corn Soup

Preparation time: 15 mins
Cooking time: 25 mins
Difficulty level: Easy
Serving: 1
PRAL: -1.8

Ingredients:

- 1 cup corn kernels
- Half onion, chopped
- 2 cups vegetable broth, low-sodium
- Pepper to taste
- 1-2 tbsp olive oil

Instructions:

- Place olive oil into the pot. Then, add onion & sauté for 3-4 mins. Add corn & sauté for 2-3 mins.
- Add vegetable broth & bring the mixture to a boil. Reduce the heat & cook for 15 to 20 mins.
- Transfer the mixture to the blender & blend until smooth.
- Season with pepper.
- Serve!

Nutrition:

Calories 150, Carbohydrate 32g, Fat 2g, Sugar 5g, Protein 3g, Potassium 500mg, Sodium 300mg, Phosphorus 120mg

Broccoli Soup

Preparation time: 10 mins
Cooking time: 45 mins
Difficulty level: Easy
Serving: 1
PRAL: -4.6

Ingredients:

- 1 cup broccoli florets
- Half onion, chopped
- 2 cups vegetable broth, low-sodium
- Pepper, to taste

Instructions:

- Add olive oil into the pot & heat it. Add onion & sauté it. Add broccoli florets & cook for 2-3 mins. Add vegetable broth & boil it. Reduce the heat & simmer for 15-20 mins.
- Add broccoli florets & cook for 2-3 mins. Place vegetable broth & bring to a boil. Reduce the heat & simmer for 15 to 20 mins.
- Transfer the mixture to the blender & blend until smooth.
- Season with pepper.
- Enjoy!

Nutrition:

Calories 50, Carbohydrate 10g, Fat 0.5g, Sugar 3g, Protein 3g, Potassium 300mg, Sodium 40mg, Phosphorus 100mg

Fish Soup

Preparation time: 10 mins
Cooking time: 15 mins
Difficulty level: Easy
Serving: 1
PRAL: 1.2

Ingredients:

- 6 oz white fish, cut into bite-sized pieces
- 2 tomatoes, chopped
- 2 celery stalks, diced
- 1 onion, chopped
- 2 cups fish or vegetable broth, low-sodium
- Pepper to taste
- Olive oil, for cooking

Instructions:

- Place olive oil into the pot. Add onion & celery & sauté for 5 mins.
- Add tomatoes & cook for 3-4 mins. Add vegetable or fish broth & bring to a boil.
- Once the broth is boiling, reduce the heat to a simmer. Add white fish pieces & saute for 5-7 mins.
- Season with pepper.
- Serve!

Nutrition:

Calories 150, Carbohydrate 8g, Fat 2g, Sugar 3g, Protein 25g, Potassium 600mg, Sodium 100mg, Phosphorus 200mg

Salmon & Barley Soup

Preparation time: 15 mins
Cooking time: 50 mins
Difficulty level: Easy
Serving: 1
PRAL: 1.6

Ingredients:

- 4 oz salmon fillet, skinless
- ½ cup barley
- 2 carrots, peeled & chopped
- 2 stalks of celery, chopped
- 4 cups chicken or vegetable broth, low-sodium
- Pepper to taste
- Olive oil, for sautéing

Instructions:

- Add water & barley into the pot & cook for 25 to 30 mins. Drain & keep it aside.
- Add olive oil into the pot & heat it. Add celery & carrots & sauté for 5 mins.
- Add broth & bring the mixture to a boil. Reduce the heat to a simmer & add cooked barley. Simmer for 15 to 20 mins.
- Season with pepper.
- Serve!

Nutrition:

Calories 250, Carbohydrate 30g, Fat 7g, Sugar 4g, Protein 20g, Potassium 400mg, Sodium 200mg, Phosphorus 200mg

Side Dishes

Spinach & Strawberry Salad

Preparation time: 15 mins
Cooking time: 0 mins
Difficulty level: Easy
Serving: 1
PRAL: -11.3

Ingredients:

- 2 cups fresh spinach leaves
- 1 cup strawberries, sliced
- ¼ cup pecans, chopped
- ¼ cup feta cheese, low-sodium, crumbled
- 2 tbsp light dressing

Instructions:

- Add strawberries & spinach into the bowl & mix well.
- Add cheese & pecans over it. Drizzle with dressing & toss well.
- Enjoy!

Nutrition:

Calories 200, Carbohydrate 16g, Fat 14g, Sugar 7g, Protein 5g, Potassium 410mg, Sodium 180mg, Phosphorus 130mg

Cauliflower Gratin

Preparation time: 15 mins
Cooking time: 35 mins
Difficulty level: Easy
Serving: 1
PRAL: -6.8

Ingredients:

- 1 head cauliflower, cut into florets
- 1 cup cheddar cheese, grated, low-sodium
- ½ cup whole wheat bread crumbs
- 2 cups skim milk
- Pepper to taste

Instructions:

- Preheat the oven to 375 degrees F.
- Steam the cauliflower florets until tender. It will take 5-7 mins. Drain & keep it aside.
- Add milk into the saucepan & heat it. Take out it from the heat.
- Add whole wheat breadcrumbs & grated cheddar cheese in another bowl & mix well.
- Layer the cauliflower into the baking dish & season with pepper.
- Pour the milk over cauliflower. Sprinkle with cheese & breadcrumb mixture.
- Bake for 20-25 mins.

Nutrition:

Calories 200, Carbohydrate 22g, Fat 7g, Sugar 7g, Protein 14g, Potassium 600mg, Sodium 150mg, Phosphorus 300mg

Lemon Asparagus

Preparation time: 1 mins
Cooking time: 15 mins
Difficulty level: Easy
Serving: 1
PRAL: -5.7

Ingredients:

- 1 bunch of fresh asparagus spears
- 1 lemon
- 2 tbsp olive oil
- Pepper, to taste

Instructions:

- Preheat the oven to 400 degrees F.
- Rinse the asparagus spears & trim the tough ends. Place the trimmed asparagus onto the baking sheet. Drizzle with olive oil. Season with pepper. Add lemon juice & roast for 12 to 15 mins.
- Serve!

Nutrition:

Calories 32, Carbohydrate 6g, Fat 2g, Sugar 2g, Protein 2g, Potassium 288mg, Sodium 2mg, Phosphorus 47mg

Green Beans with Almonds

Preparation time: 5 mins
Cooking time: 10 mins
Difficulty level: Easy
Serving: 1
PRAL: -4.9

Ingredients:

- 1 pound green beans, trimmed
- ¼ cup almonds, sliced
- 2 tbsp olive oil
- Pepper, to taste

Instructions:

- Add water into the pot & boil it. Add salt & green beans & boil for 3-4 mins. Drain & transfer it to a bowl of ice water.
- Add olive oil into the intermediate skillet & heat it. Add almonds & sauté for 2-3 mins.
- Add green beans & toss them in the olive oil & almond mixture & sauté for 2-3 mins.
- Season with pepper.

Nutrition:

Calories 120, Carbohydrate 9g, Fat 9g, Sugar 2g, Protein 3g, Potassium 240mg, Sodium 100mg, Phosphorus 50mg

Quinoa Salad with Grilled Vegetables

Preparation time: 10 mins
Cooking time: 25 mins
Difficulty level: Easy
Serving: 1
PRAL: -8.1

Ingredients:

- Half cup quinoa
- 1 zucchini, sliced
- 1 red bell pepper, sliced
- 1 small eggplant, sliced
- 2 tbsp olive oil
- 1 tsp lemon juice
- Pepper, to taste

Instructions:

- Rinse the quinoa under cold running water. Add ½ cup of quinoa & 1 cup of water into the saucepan & boil & simmer for 15 mins. Remove from heat.
- Preheat the grill to medium-high heat.
- Add pepper, salt, 1 tbsp of olive oil, eggplant, red bell pepper, & zucchini into the bowl & toss well. Grill for 3-4 mins per side.
- Remove from grill.
- Prepare the dressing: Add pepper, olive oil, & lemon juice into the bowl & whisk to combine.
- Add grilled vegetables & cooked quinoa into the bowl. Pour dressing over salad. Toss together.
- Enjoy!

Nutrition:

Calories 200, Carbohydrate 45g, Fat 12g, Sugar 5g, Protein 8g, Potassium 400mg, Sodium 300mg, Phosphorus 200mg

Mashed Sweet Potatoes

Preparation time: 5 mins
Cooking time: 20 mins
Difficulty level: Easy
Serving: 1
PRAL: -5.3

Ingredients:

- 2 lbs sweet potatoes
- ½ cup almond milk, unsweetened
- ½ tsp ground cinnamon
- Pepper, as desired

Instructions:

- Rinse & peel the sweet potatoes. Then, cut into chunks.
- Add potato chunks into the pot & cover with water.
- Reduce the heat to simmer & cook for 15-20 mins.
- Drain & return them to the pot. Mash the sweet potato with a potato masher.
- Add cinnamon & almond milk into the bowl & combine together.
- Season with pepper.
- Serve!

Nutrition:

Calories 90, Carbohydrate 21g, Fat 0g, Sugar 5g, Protein 1g, Potassium 300mg, Sodium 50mg, Phosphorus 40mg

Mushroom Stuffed Zucchini

Preparation time: 15 mins
Cooking time: 50 mins
Difficulty level: Easy
Serving: 1
PRAL: -7.2

Ingredients:

- 4 zucchinis
- 2 cups mushrooms, chopped
- 1 onion
- 2 tbsp parsley, chopped
- 4 oz feta cheese, low-sodium
- Olive oil, for sautéing
- Pepper, to taste

Instructions:

- Preheat the oven to 375 degrees F.
- Rinse the zucchini & cut them into lengthwise. Scoop out the flesh.
- Add olive oil into the pot & heat it. Add chopped onion & cook for 3-4 mins.
- Add zucchini flesh & mushroom & sauté for 5-7 mins. Remove the pot from the heat. Then, add pepper, feta, & chopped parsley & stir well.
- Stuff the zucchini half with mushroom mixture. Place the stuffed zucchini halves onto the baking sheet. Bake for 25 to 30 mins.
- Serve!

Nutrition:

Calories 110, Carbohydrate 10g, Fat 6g, Sugar 4g, Protein 5g, Potassium 300mg, Sodium 100mg, Phosphorus 120mg

Couscous with Raisins & Almonds

Preparation time: 5 mins
Cooking time: 10 mins
Difficulty level: Easy
Serving: 1
PRAL: 1.2

Ingredients:

- 1 cup whole wheat couscous
- ½ cup raisins
- ¼ cup almonds, sliced
- 2 tbsp fresh parsley, chopped

Instructions:

- Add 1 ¼ cups of water into the pot & boil it.
- Add couscous into the heat-proof bowl. Add boiled water over it. Cover the bowl with a lid. Allow it sit for 5 mins. Fluff the couscous with a fork.
- Add parsley, almonds, & raisins into the couscous & mix well.
- Serve!

Nutrition:

Calories 250, Carbohydrate 55g, Fat 6g, Sugar 10g, Protein 8g, Potassium 150mg, Sodium 5mg, Phosphorus 150mg

Beet & Walnut Salad

Preparation time: 15 mins
Cooking time: 1 hr
Difficulty level: Easy
Serving: 1
PRAL: 1.4

Ingredients:

- 2 beets
- ½ cup walnuts, chopped
- ¼ cup goat cheese, low-sodium, crumbled
- 2 tbsp balsamic vinegar
- 2 tbsp olive oil
- Pepper, to taste

Instructions:

- Preheat the oven to 400 degrees F.
- Place the beets onto the baking dish & roast for 1 hour until tender.
- Peel & slice them into thin rounds.
- Add walnuts into the skillet & heat it. Keep it aside.
- Prepare the dressing: Add olive oil & balsamic vinegar into the bowl & mix well. Add pepper & stir well.
- Assemble the salad: Add beet into the bowl & sprinkle with cheese & toasted walnuts.
- Pour dressing and mix together.
- Serve!

Nutrition:

Calories 300, Carbohydrate 20g, Fat 20g, Sugar 10g, Protein 7g, Potassium 500mg, Sodium 150mg, Phosphorus 150mg

Roasted Potatoes with Rosemary

Preparation Time: 10 minutes
Cooking Time: 25 minutes
Difficulty level: Medium
Serving: 1
PRAL (Potential Renal Acid Load): -6.2

Ingredients:

- 1 medium-sized potato, washed and diced
- 1 tablespoon olive oil
- 1 teaspoon fresh rosemary, finely chopped
- Black pepper to taste

Instructions:

- Preheat your oven to 400°F (200°C).
- In a bowl, toss the diced potatoes with olive oil, chopped rosemary, and black pepper until the potatoes are evenly coated.
- Spread the potatoes in a single layer on a baking sheet.
- Roast in the preheated oven for about 25 minutes or until the potatoes are golden brown and crispy on the edges, turning them halfway through for even cooking.
- Once done, remove from the oven and let them cool for a few minutes before serving.

Nutrition:

Calories: 200 kcal, Carbohydrates: 25g, Fat: 10g, Sugar: 1g, Protein: 2g, Potassium: 600mg, Sodium: 150mg, Phosphorus: 80mg

Salads

Spinach & Blueberry Salad

Preparation time: 5 mins
Cooking time: 0 mins
Difficulty level: Easy
Serving: 1
PRAL: -5.9

Ingredients:

- 2 cups fresh spinach
- ½ cup blueberries
- ¼ cup walnuts, chopped
- 1 oz feta cheese, low-sodium
- 1 tbsp balsamic vinegar

Instructions:

- Rinse & dry the spinach leaves. Then, tear them into pieces.
- Add blueberries & spinach into the salad bowl & mix well. Add chopped walnuts & feta cheese over it. Drizzle with balsamic vinegar. Serve!

Nutrition:

Calories 250, Carbohydrate 18g, Fat 18g, Sugar 6g, Protein 8g, Potassium 500mg, Sodium 280mg, Phosphorus 150mg

Basmati Rice Salad with Vegetables

Preparation time: 15 mins
Cooking time: 20 mins
Difficulty level: Easy
Serving: 1
PRAL: -6.5

Ingredients:

- 1 cup Basmati rice
- ½ cup peas
- ½ cup carrots, diced
- ¼ cup onion, chopped
- 2 tbsp parsley
- 1 tsp lemon juice
- Pepper to taste

Instructions:

- Rinse the rice & add it to the pot with 2 cups of water & boil it. Cover with a lid. Simmer for 15 to 20 mins. Fluff with a fork.
- Add water into the pot & heat it. Add peas & carrots & cook for 2-3 mins. Drain & run under cold water.
- Add parsley, onion, carrot, peas, & cooked balsamic rice into the mixing bowl & mix well. Add lemon juice over it. Toss well.
- Season with pepper.
- Serve!

Nutrition:

Calories 180, Carbohydrate 40g, Fat 1g, Sugar 3g, Protein 4g, Potassium 200mg, Sodium 200mg, Phosphorus 80mg

Greek Salad

Preparation time: 10 mins
Cooking time: 0 mins
Difficulty level: Easy
Serving: 1
PRAL: -4.7

Ingredients:

- 2 cucumbers
- 4 tomatoes
- ½ cup black olives, low-sodium
- ½ cup feta cheese, low-sodium
- 1 tsp dried oregano
- 2 tbsp olive oil

Instructions:

- Add cucumber, feta cheese, & olives into the decent salad bowl. Sprinkle with dried oregano & olive oil. Toss well.

Nutrition:

Calories 220, Carbohydrate 10g, Fat 16g, Sugar 4g, Protein 6g, Potassium 300mg, Sodium 250mg, Phosphorus 150mg

Avocado & Mango Salad

Preparation time: 10 mins
Cooking time: 0 mins
Difficulty level: Easy
Serving: 1
PRAL: -4.3

Ingredients:

- 1 ripe avocado, diced
- 1 ripe mango, diced
- 2 cups of lettuce, washed & cut into pieces
- ¼ cup almonds, sliced
- One tsp lemon juice
- Pepper, to taste

Instructions:

- Prepare the salad dressing: Add black pepper & lemon juice into the bowl.
- Add almonds, mango, & avocado into the salad bowl & mix together.
- Pour lemon dressing over salad & toss well.
- Add washed & torn lettuce & toss well.
- Serve!

Nutrition:

Calories 250, Carbohydrate 23g, Fat 17g, Sugar 11g, Protein 4g, Potassium 760mg, Sodium 150mg, Phosphorus 100mg

Lentil & Spinach Salad

Preparation time: 10 mins
Cooking time: 0 mins
Difficulty level: Easy
Serving: 1
PRAL: -6.1

Ingredients:

- Half cup lentils, cooked
- 2 cups fresh spinach, washed & chopped
- ¼ cup red onion, thinly sliced
- 1 tbsp apple cider vinegar
- Pepper, to taste

Instructions:

- Add water into the pot & boil it. Add lentils & cook for 20-25 mins until tender. Drain & allow it cool.
- Add red onion, spinach, & cooked lentils into the bowl & mix well.
- Drizzle with apple cider vinegar.
- Serve!

Nutrition:

Calories 150, Carbohydrate 28g, Fat 1g, Sugar 2g, Protein 10g, Potassium 430mg, Sodium 150mg, Phosphorus 160mg

Beet & Mint Salad

Preparation time: 15 mins
Cooking time: 40 mins
Difficulty level: Easy
Serving: 1
PRAL: -2.8

Ingredients:

- 3 beets
- ¼ cup fresh mint leaves, chopped
- 2 tbsp balsamic vinegar

Instructions:

- Add water into the pot & boil it. Add beets & cook for 30-40 mins.
- Then, peel & cut them into small cubes.
- Add beet cubes & mint leaves into the bowl & mix well.
- Add balsamic vinegar over beet & mint mixture. Toss well.
- Serve!

Nutrition:

Calories 75, Carbohydrate 17g, Fat 0g, Sugar 11g, Protein 2g, Potassium 455mg, Sodium 45mg, Phosphorus 40mg

Brussels Sprout & Tangerine Salad

Preparation time: 15 mins
Cooking time: 0 mins
Difficulty level: Easy
Serving: 1
PRAL: -3.6

Ingredients:

- 12-14 Brussels sprouts, shredded
- 2-3 tangerines
- ½ cup walnuts
- 2 tbsp apple cider vinegar
- Pepper, to taste

Instructions:

- Add walnuts into the frying pan & toast it. Then, chop it.
- Add shredded Brussels sprouts, chopped walnuts, & tangerine segments into the bowl & mix well. Drizzle with apple cider vinegar & toss well.
- Serve!

Nutrition:

Calories 200, Carbohydrate 25g, Fat 10g, Sugar 12g, Protein 6g, Potassium 600mg, Sodium 45mg, Phosphorus 150mg

Black Bean & Corn Salad

Preparation time: 15 mins
Cooking time: 0 mins
Difficulty level: Easy
Serving: 1
PRAL: 1.5

Ingredients:

- 15 oz black beans, drained & rinsed
- 1 cup frozen corn kernels, thawed
- Half red onion, diced
- ¼ cup of fresh cilantro, chopped
- 1 tsp lime juice
- Pepper, to taste

Instructions:

- Add cilantro, red onion, corn, & black beans into the mixing bowl & mix well.
- Add lime juice over salad & toss well.
- Season with pepper.
- Place it into the fridge for 30 mins.
- Serve!

Nutrition:

Calories 150, Carbohydrate 30g, Fat 1g, Sugar 2g, Protein 6g, Potassium 350mg, Sodium 200mg, Phosphorus 100mg

Quinoa & Chickpea Salad

Preparation time: 15 mins
Cooking time: 0 mins
Difficulty level: Easy
Serving: 1
PRAL: 1.2

Ingredients:

- 1 cup quinoa
- 1 ½ cups chickpeas, cooked
- 1 cucumber, diced
- ½ cup fresh parsley, chopped
- 1 tsp lemon juice
- Pepper to taste

Instructions:

- Add two cups of water into the medium pot & boil it. Add quinoa & simmer for 15 mins. Then, fluff with a fork.
- Add parsley, cucumber, chickpeas, & cooked quinoa into the bowl & mix well.
- Add lemon juice over salad. Season with pepper.
- Serve!

Nutrition:

Calories 320, Carbohydrate 57g, Fat 5g, Sugar 4g, Protein 13g, Potassium 400mg, Sodium 200mg, Phosphorus 290mg

Tomato and Cucumber Salad

Preparation time: 5 minutes
Cooking time: 0 minutes
Difficulty level: Easy
Serving: 1
PRAL: -4.2

Ingredients:

- 2 tomatoes, diced
- 2 cucumbers, diced
- Half red onion, chopped
- 2 tbsp red wine vinegar
- 2 tbsp olive oil

Instructions:

- Add red onion, cucumber, and diced tomatoes into the bowl and mix well.
- Add olive oil, and red wine vinegar in another bowl and mix well.
- Pour the dressing over salad and toss well.
- Allow it to stand for 10-15 minutes.
- Enjoy!

Nutrition:

Calories 100, Carbohydrate 10g, Fat 6g, Sugar 4g, Protein 2g, Potassium 300mg, Sodium 100mg, Phosphorus 40mg

Snacks

Avocado Salsa with Corn Tortillas

Preparation time: 15 mins
Cooking time: 5 mins
Difficulty level: Easy
Serving: 1
PRAL: -4.6

Ingredients:

- 2 ripe avocados
- 1 tomato, diced
- ¼ cup red onion, chopped
- ¼ cup fresh cilantro, chopped
- 4 corn tortillas
- Pepper, to taste

Instructions:

- Add avocado flesh into the bowl & mash well. Add cilantro, red onion, & tomato & mix well. Season with pepper.
- Heat a dry skillet over medium heat.
- Place the corn tortilla & cook for 30 seconds.
- Place the mixture over corn tortilla.
- Serve!

Nutrition:

Calories 180, Carbohydrate 26g, Fat 9g, Sugar 2g, Protein 3g, Potassium 570mg, Sodium 160mg, Phosphorus 70mg

Fresh Fruit Salad

Preparation time: 10 mins
Cooking time: 0 mins
Difficulty level: Easy
Serving: 1
PRAL: -4.8

Ingredients:

- 1 cup strawberries, sliced
- 1 cup blueberries
- 2 peaches, peeled & diced
- 1 tsp lemon juice

Instructions:

- Add all fruits into the mixing bowl & toss together.
- Add lemon juice & toss well.
- Serve!

Nutrition:

Calories 60, Carbohydrate 15g, Fat 0g, Sugar 10g, Protein 1g, Potassium 180mg, Sodium 0mg, Phosphorus 20mg

Cucumber Salad with Yogurt & Dill

Preparation time: 30 mins
Cooking time: 0 mins
Difficulty level: Easy
Serving: 1
PRAL: -3.5

Ingredients:

- Two cucumbers
- 1 cup Greek yogurt, low-fat
- 2 tbsp fresh dill, chopped
- Pepper, as desired

Instructions:

- Add cucumber into the medium bowl.
- Add dill, pepper, & yogurt in another bowl & whisk together.
- Pour this mixture over cucumber & toss well.
- Place it into the fridge for 30 mins.
- Serve!

Nutrition:

Calories 100, Carbohydrate 15g, Fat 1g, Sugar 6g, Protein 10g, Potassium 300mg, Sodium 60mg, Phosphorus 120mg

Baked Sweet Potatoes with Cinnamon

Preparation time: 15 mins
Cooking time: 30 mins
Difficulty level: Medium
Serving: 1
PRAL: -5.1

Ingredients:

- 4 sweet potatoes
- 1 tsp ground cinnamon
- 2 tbsp olive oil

Instructions:

- Preheat the oven to 400 degrees F.
- Add sliced sweet potatoes into the bowl. Add olive oil & cinnamon & toss well.
- Place seasoned potato onto the baking sheet. Bake for 25 to 30 mins.
- Serve!

Nutrition:

Calories 200, Carbohydrate 35g, Fat 7g, Sugar 8g, Protein 2g, Potassium 600mg, Sodium 150mg, Phosphorus 60mg

Yogurt Sauce

Preparation time: 30 mins
Cooking time: 0 mins
Difficulty level: Easy
Serving: 1
PRAL: -3.2

Ingredients:

- 1 cup low-fat Greek yogurt
- ½ cup bell peppers, chopped
- ½ cup carrots, chopped
- ½ cup celery, chopped

Instructions:

- Add celery, carrots, yogurt, & bell pepper into the mixing bowl & mix well.
- Place the sauce into the fridge for 30 mins.
- Serve!

Nutrition:

Calories 25, Carbohydrate 3g, Fat 0g, Sugar 2g, Protein 2g, Potassium 88mg, Sodium 25mg, Phosphorus 35mg

Guacamole with Corn Chips

Preparation time: 15 mins
Cooking time: 0 mins
Difficulty level: Easy
Serving: 1
PRAL: -3.8

Ingredients:

- 2 ripe avocados
- 1 lemon
- 1 tomato
- Corn tortillas or corn chips

Instructions:

- Add avocado flesh into the mixing bowl & mash it well. Add lemon juice & diced tomatoes & toss well.
- Season with pepper.
- Serve with corn tortillas.

Nutrition:

Calories 120, Carbohydrate 7g, Fat 11g, Sugar 1g, Protein 1g, Potassium 375mg, Sodium 7mg, Phosphorus 36mg

Walnut & Blueberry Muffins

Preparation time: 5 mins
Cooking time: 30 mins
Difficulty level: Medium
Serving: 1
PRAL: 2.1

Ingredients:

- 1 ½ cups whole wheat flour
- ½ cup walnuts, chopped
- 1 cup fresh blueberries
- 2 eggs
- ½ cup sugar
- ½ cup milk
- ¼ cup vegetable oil
- 1 ½ tsp baking powder
- ½ tsp baking soda
- 1 tsp vanilla extract

Instructions:

- Firstly, preheat the oven to 350 degrees F.
- Line the muffin tin with paper liners.
- Add vanilla, vegetable oil, milk, sugar, & eggs into the mixing bowl & whisk to combine.
- Add baking soda, baking powder, walnuts, & flour in another bowl & mix well.
- Add dry ingredients to the wet ingredients & mix well. Fold in blueberries.
- Divide the batter into the muffin cups. Bake for 20 to 25 mins.
- Serve!

Nutrition:

Calories 200, Carbohydrate 25g, Fat 10g, Sugar 8g, Protein 5g, Potassium 150mg, Sodium 150mg, Phosphorus 150mg

Apple & Cinnamon Muffins

Preparation time: 10 mins
Cooking time: 25 mins
Difficulty level: Medium
Serving: 1
PRAL: 2.3

Ingredients:

- 1 cup whole wheat flour
- 2 apples, peeled, cored, & diced
- 1 tsp ground cinnamon
- 2 eggs

Instructions:

- Preheat the oven to 350 degrees F.
- Line a muffin tin with paper liners.
- Add ground cinnamon & flour into the mixing bowl & mix well.
- Place eggs in another bowl & beat well.
- Add beaten egg into the dry ingredients.
- Fold in diced apples. Pour batter into the muffin cups & bake for 20 to 25 mins.
- Serve!

Nutrition:

Calories 120, Carbohydrate 20g, Fat 2g, Sugar 6g, Protein 4g, Potassium 150mg, Sodium 90mg, Phosphorus 90mg

Cucumber & Tomato Salad

Preparation time: 5 mins
Cooking time: 0 mins
Difficulty level: Easy
Serving: 1
PRAL: -4.2

Ingredients:

- 2 cucumbers, sliced
- 4 tomatoes, diced
- Half red onion, thinly sliced
- ¼ cup fresh parsley, chopped
- 2 tbsp red wine vinegar

Instructions:

- Prepare all ingredients: Rinse, peel, & slice the cucumber. Dice the tomatoes. Thinly slice the red onion. Chop the parsley.
- Add parsley, red onion, tomatoes, & cucumber into the bowl & mix well.
- Add red wine vinegar over the salad. Toss well.
- Season with pepper.
- Serve!

Nutrition:

Calories 50, Carbohydrate 12g, Fat 0g, Sugar 6g, Protein 2g, Potassium 350mg, Sodium 15mg, Phosphorus 45mg

Chickpea Hummus with Fresh Vegetables

Preparation time: 15 mins
Cooking time: 0 mins
Difficulty level: Easy
Serving: 1
PRAL: -2.3

Ingredients:

- 1 ½ cups chickpeas, cooked
- ¼ cup olive oil
- 2 cloves garlic
- 1 tsp lemon juice
- 2 carrots, sliced into sticks
- Two celery stalks, sliced into sticks
- Pepper, to taste

Instructions:

- Add lemon juice, garlic, olive oil, & cooked chickpeas into the blender & blend until smooth.
- Season with pepper.
- Serve!

Nutrition:

Calories 200, Carbohydrate 20g, Fat 11g, Sugar 2g, Protein 6g, Potassium 230mg, Sodium 200mg, Phosphorus 200mg

Desserts

Blueberry & Strawberry Ice Cream

Preparation time: 4 hours
Cooking time: 0 mins
Difficulty level: Easy
Serving: 1
PRAL: -3.4

Ingredients:

- 2 ripe blueberry
- 1 cup strawberries
- ½ cup whipping cream, low-fat
- 1 tbsp sugar

Instructions:

- Add strawberries & blueberry into the blender & mix & mix. Add whipping cream & sugar & blend until smooth.
- Place it into the fridge for 4 hrs.
- Serve!

Nutrition:

Calories 170, Carbohydrate 40g, Fat 2g, Sugar 21g, Protein 2g, Potassium 450mg, Sodium 10mg, Phosphorus 70mg

Sugar-Free Apple Pie

Preparation time: 10 mins
Cooking time: 1 hour
Difficulty level: Medium
Serving: 1
PRAL: -3.7

Ingredients:

- 4-5 apples, peeled, cored, & sliced
- 1 cup almond flour
- 1 tsp ground cinnamon
- 2 tbsp lemon juice

Instructions:

- Preheat the oven to 350 degrees F.
- Add cinnamon, lemon juice & apple into the bowl & mix well.
- Add almond flour in another bowl.
- Grease the pie dish with butter.
- Spread the almond flour mixture into the dish. Add seasoned apple slices over it.
- Add remaining almond flour mixture over apples. Cover with foil. Bake for 30-40 mins.
- Take out the foil & bake for 10-15 mins.
- Serve!

Nutrition:

Calories 170, Carbohydrate 18g, Fat 11g, Sugar 0g, Protein 4g, Potassium 180mg, Sodium 20mg, Phosphorus 100mg

Chia Pudding with Berries

Preparation time: 2 hours
Cooking time: 0 mins
Difficulty level: Easy
Serving: 1
PRAL: -4.2

Ingredients:

- 2 tbsp chia seeds
- 1 cup unsweetened almond milk
- ½ cup mixed berries, strawberries, blueberries, raspberries

Instructions:

- Add almond milk & chia seeds into the mixing bowl & mix well. Allow the mixture sit for a few mins.
- Place it into the fridge for 2 hours.
- Top with mixed berries.
- Serve!

Nutrition:

Calories 180, Carbohydrate 16g, Fat 11g, Sugar 2g, Protein 6g, Potassium 180mg, Sodium 100mg, Phosphorus 100mg

Coconut Cream with Pineapple

Preparation time: 15 mins
Cooking time: 0 mins
Difficulty level: Easy
Serving: 1
PRAL: -4.8

Ingredients:

- 1 cup coconut milk
- One cup fresh pineapple chunks
- Sweetener, low-carb

Instructions:

- Add the coconut milk & fresh pineapple chunks into the blender & mix & mix.
- Add sweetener & stir well.
- Pour coconut cream with pineapple into the bowl.
- Serve!

Nutrition:

Calories 150, Carbohydrate 15g, Fat 10g, Sugar 5g, Protein 1g, Potassium 200mg, Sodium 10mg, Phosphorus 10mg

Caramelized Pears

Preparation time: 5 mins
Cooking time: 10 mins
Difficulty level: Easy
Serving: 1
PRAL: -4.1

Ingredients:

- 4 pears, peeled, cored, & sliced
- 2-3 tbsp low-sugar sweetener
- ½ tsp ground cinnamon

Instructions:

- Place olive oil into the skillet & heat it.
- Add sliced pears & ground cinnamon & stir well.
- Drizzle with sweetener.
- Add coated pears & cook for 5-7 mins.
- Serve!

Nutrition:

Calories 100, Carbohydrate 26g, Fat 10g, Sugar 16g, Protein 1g, Potassium 190mg, Sodium 100mg, Phosphorus 10mg

Lemon Mousse

Preparation time: 1-2 hours
Cooking time: 0 mins
Difficulty level: Easy
Serving: 1
PRAL: -2.9

Ingredients:

- 1 cup low-fat Greek yogurt
- 1 tsp lemon zest
- 2-3 tbsp sweetener

Instructions:

- Add lemon zest & Greek yogurt into the bowl & mix well.
- Add sweetener & stir well.
- Divide the lemon mousse into glasses.
- Place it into the fridge for 1-2 hours.
- Serve!

Nutrition:

Calories 90, Carbohydrate 8g, Fat 2g, Sugar 6g, Protein 10g, Potassium 150mg, Sodium 40mg, Phosphorus 100mg

Oatmeal & Apricot Cakes

Preparation time: 15 mins
Cooking time: 20 mins
Difficulty level: Medium
Serving: 1
PRAL: -2.7

Ingredients:

- 1 cup oatmeal
- ½ cup dried apricots
- 2 eggs

Instructions:

- Firstly, preheat the oven to 350 degrees F.
- Apply the butter onto the baking dish.
- Add dried apricots & oatmeal into the blender & blend until smooth.
- Add eggs into the mixing bowl & beat well.
- Add oatmeal & apricot mixture to the eggs & stir well.
- Divide the dough into portions. Shape the mixture into cookies or cakes.
- Place onto the medium baking dish & bake for 12 to 15 mins.
- Serve!

Nutrition:

Calories 80, Carbohydrate 12g, Fat 2g, Sugar 4g, Protein 3g, Potassium 150mg, Sodium 20mg, Phosphorus 80mg

Strawberry Cheesecake

Preparation time: 10 mins
Cooking time: 0 mins
Difficulty level: Easy
Serving: 1
PRAL: 1.8

Ingredients:

- 1 ½ cups spreadable cheese, low-fat
- 1 cup fresh strawberries, sliced
- ¼ cup low-sugar sweetener

Instructions:

- Add sweetener & cheese into the mixing bowl & mix well.
- Press it into the pie dish. Pour the cheesecake mixture onto the crust.
- Add strawberries over cheesecake mixture. Place the mixture into the fridge for a few hours.
- Serve!

Nutrition:

Calories 130, Carbohydrate 9g, Fat 7g, Sugar 4g, Protein 6g, Potassium 135mg, Sodium 250mg, Phosphorus 80mg

Chocolate Almond Muffins

Preparation time: 10 mins
Cooking time: 20 mins
Difficulty level: Medium
Serving: 1
PRAL: 2.5

Ingredients:

- 1 cup almond flour
- ¼ cup cocoa powder
- 2 eggs
- Sweetener, to taste
- Baking powder

Instructions:

- Preheat the oven to 350 degrees F.
- Line a muffin tin with paper liners.
- Add cocoa powder & almond flour into the mixing bowl & mix well.
- Crack the eggs into the dry mixture & stir well.
- Pour the batter into the muffin cups. Bake for 15 to 20 mins.
- Serve!

Nutrition:

Calories 150, Carbohydrate 6g, Fat 12g, Sugar 1g, Protein 6g, Potassium 150mg, Sodium 40mg, Phosphorus 150mg

Caffeine-Free Tiramisu

Preparation time: 10 mins
Cooking time: 0 mins
Difficulty level: Easy
Serving: 1
PRAL: 1.9

Ingredients:

- 1 cup mascarpone cheese
- Sugar-free cookies
- Cocoa powder, for dusting
- 2 tbsp sugar

Instructions:

- Add sugar & mascarpone cheese into the mixing bowl.
- Prepare the tiramisu: Add cookies into the dish. Add half of mascarpone mixture over cookies.
- Add another layer of cookies on top of the mascarpone mixture.
- Add the remaining mascarpone mixture & spread it.
- Dust the top with cocoa powder.
- Place it into the fridge for a few hours.
- Serve!

Nutrition:

Calories 250, Carbohydrate 10g, Fat 20g, Sugar 1g, Protein 5g, Potassium 150mg, Sodium 40mg, Phosphorus 150mg

Bonus Chapter Low-Carb

Breakfast Recipes

Baked Eggs with Avocado

Preparation time: 10 mins
Cooking time: 20 mins
Difficulty level: Medium
Serving: 1
PRAL: -2.8 (negative)

Ingredients:

- 2 eggs
- 1 avocado
- ¼ cup cheddar cheese, grated
- Pepper, to taste

Instructions:

- Preheat the oven to 425 degrees F.
- Place the avocado halves onto the baking dish.
- Crack one egg into the avocado half.
- Sprinkle with grated cheddar cheese.
- Season with pepper.
- Place the baking dish into the oven & bake for 15 to 20 mins.
- Serve!

Nutrition:

Calories 350, Carbohydrate 5g, Fat 30g, Sugar 1g, Protein 12g, Potassium 700mg, Sodium 200mg, Phosphorus 200mg

Cucumber & Spinach Smoothie

Preparation time: 10 mins
Cooking time: 0 mins
Difficulty level: Easy
Serving: 1
PRAL: -4.5 (negative)

Ingredients:

- One cucumber, chopped
- 2 cups fresh spinach leaves
- ½ cup Greek yogurt, unsweetened
- 1 tbsp lemon juice

Instructions:

- Add Greek yogurt, cucumber, & spinach leaves into the blender & blend until smooth.
- Serve!

Nutrition:

Calories 90, Carbohydrate 10g, Fat 2g, Sugar 3g, Protein 7g, Potassium 600mg, Sodium 50mg, Phosphorus 150mg

Grilled Eggplant with Sun-Dried Tomatoes

Preparation time: 5 mins
Cooking time: 10 mins
Difficulty level: Medium
Serving: 1
PRAL: -2.3 (negative)

Ingredients:

- 1 eggplant
- ¼ cup sun-dried tomatoes in oil, drained & chopped
- 2 cloves garlic, minced
- Olive oil, for grilling & seasoning
- Pepper, to taste

Instructions:

- Preheat the grill to medium-high heat.
- Place the eggplant slices onto the grill & cook for 3-4 mins per side.
- Add olive oil into the pan & heat it. Add tomato & garlic & sauté for 1-2 mins.
- Serve!

Nutrition:

Calories 150, Carbohydrate 12g, Fat 11g, Sugar 5g, Protein 2g, Potassium 400mg, Sodium 200mg, Phosphorus 50mg

Zucchini Carpaccio with Ricotta

Preparation time: 10 mins
Cooking time: 0 mins
Difficulty level: Easy
Serving: 1
PRAL: -1.7 (negative)

Ingredients:

- 2 zucchinis
- ½ cup fresh ricotta cheese
- ¼ cup fresh mint leaves
- 2 tbsp olive oil
- Pepper to taste

Instructions:

- Prepare the vinaigrette: Add pepper & olive oil into the bowl & mix well.
- Drizzle vinaigrette over zucchini slices. Top with cheese. Season with pepper.
- Serve!

Nutrition:

Calories 150, Carbohydrate 4g, Fat 11g, Sugar 2g, Protein 6g, Potassium 300mg, Sodium 200mg, Phosphorus 150mg

Zucchini Spaghetti with Shrimp & Parsley Pesto

Preparation time: 10 mins
Cooking time: 10 mins
Difficulty level: Medium
Serving: 1
PRAL: -3.2 (negative)

Ingredients:

- 2 zucchinis
- 12 shrimp, peeled & deveined
- 1 cup fresh parsley leaves
- 2 cloves of garlic
- 2 tbsp olive oil
- Pepper to taste

Instructions:

- Cut the zucchini with a julienne peeler & season with pepper.
- Squeeze the zucchini to remove the excess liquid.
- Add olive oil, garlic cloves, & parsley into the blender & blend until smooth.
- Add olive oil into the skillet & heat it.
- Season the shrimp with pepper. Add them to the skillet & cook for 1-2 mins per side.
- Add zucchini spaghetti into the same skillet & cook for 2-3 mins.
- Add parsley pesto & toss well.
- Serve!

Nutrition:

Calories 250, Carbohydrate 10g, Fat 13g, Sugar 3g, Protein 25g, Potassium 500mg, Sodium 100mg, Phosphorus 150mg

Seafood Salad with Lemon & Avocado

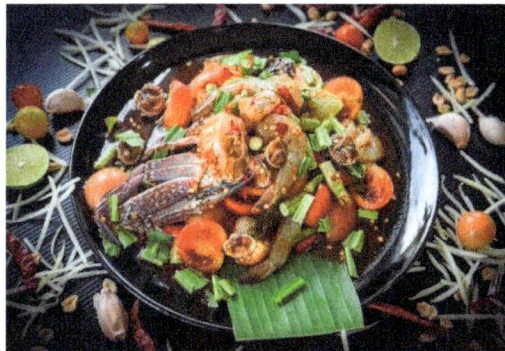

Preparation time: 20 mins
Cooking time: 0 mins
Difficulty level: Easy
Serving: 1
PRAL: -2.8 (negative)

Ingredients:

- 8-10 shrimp, cooked
- 1 cup octopus, cooked
- One tsp lemon juice
- One ripe avocado
- 2 tbsp fresh parsley, chopped
- Pepper, as desired

Instructions:

- Cut the cooked octopus into pieces.
- Add cooked shrimp, octopus, avocado, lemon zest, & parsley into the bowl & combine well.

Nutrition:

Calories 250, Carbohydrate 12g, Fat 13g, Sugar 1g, Protein 23g, Potassium 620mg, Sodium 150mg, Phosphorus 200mg

Land First Courses

Zoodles with Basil Pesto & Cherry Tomatoes

Preparation time: 10 mins
Cooking time: 0 mins
Difficulty level: Easy
Serving: 1
PRAL: -3.8 (negative)

Ingredients:

- 2 zucchinis
- 2 cups fresh basil leaves
- ½ cup cherry tomatoes
- ¼ cup pine nuts
- ¼ cup olive oil
- Pepper to taste

Instructions:

- Cut the zucchini into noodles with vegetable peeler.
- Add olive oil, nuts, & basil leaves into the blender & blend until smooth.
- Season with pepper.
- Add cherry tomato into the skillet & cook for a few mins. Drizzle with olive oil. Sprinkle with pepper.
- Add basil pesto & zucchini noodles into the medium bowl & toss well.
- Serve!

Nutrition:

Calories 250, Carbohydrate 11g, Fat 22g, Sugar 5g, Protein 4g, Potassium 480mg, Sodium 90mg, Phosphorus 100mg

Stuffed Mushrooms with Ricotta & Walnuts

Preparation time: 10 mins
Cooking time: 30 mins
Difficulty level: Medium
Serving: 1
PRAL: -3.4 (negative)

Ingredients:

- 1 cup mushrooms
- 1 tbsp ricotta cheese
- 1 tbsp walnuts, chopped
- 1 tsp thyme
- Olive oil, for drizzling
- Pepper, as desired

Instructions:

- Firstly, preheat the oven to 375 degrees F.
- Clean the mushroom with damp cloth & remove the dirt. Remove the stems from the mushrooms, creating a hollow space in each cap. Keep it aside.
- Chop the mushroom & add them into the mixing bowl.
- Add chopped mushrooms, ricotta cheese, thyme, & walnuts into the bowl & mix together. Season with pepper. Take each mushroom cap & stuff it with ricotta & mushroom mixture. Sprinkle with olive oil. Bake for 20 to 25 mins.
- Serve!

Nutrition:

Calories 60, Carbohydrate 2g, Fat 4g, Sugar 1g, Protein 3g, Potassium 120mg, Sodium 50mg, Phosphorus 50m

Seafood Main Courses

Grilled Tuna with Lemon & Caper Sauce

Preparation time: 10 mins
Cooking time: 10 mins
Difficulty level: Medium
Serving: 1
PRAL: -3.1 (negative)

Ingredients:

- 6 oz tuna fillet
- 1 tsp lemon juice
- 1 tbsp capers
- 1 tbsp olive oil
- Pepper, to taste

Instructions:

- Preheat the grill to medium-high heat.
- Season the fillet with pepper & salt. Add lemon juice over it.
- Grill for 2-3 mins per side.
- Prepare the sauce: Add olive oil into the saucepan & heat it. Add capers & sauté for 1 minute.
- Remove the saucepan from the heat. Add lemon juice & stir well.
- Add sauce over cooked tuna.
- Serve!

Nutrition:

Calories 220, Carbohydrate 2g, Fat 9g, Sugar 0g, Protein 32g, Potassium 460mg, Sodium 540mg, Phosphorus 250mg

Cartoccio Sole with Olives & Cherry Tomatoes

Preparation time: 10 mins
Cooking time: 20 mins
Difficulty level: Medium
Serving: 1
PRAL: -2.7 (negative)

Ingredients:

- 4 sole fillets
- ½ cup black olives, pitted
- 1 cup cherry tomatoes, halved
- 4 cloves garlic, minced
- 2 tbsp fresh parsley, chopped
- Pepper to taste
- Olive oil, for drizzling

Instructions:

- Preheat the oven to 375 degrees F.
- Place the sole fillets onto the foil. Spread the garlic, cherry tomatoes, & olives among the fillets & drizzle with olive oil.
- Fold & seal the foil around the fish to create packet.
- Place the foil onto the baking sheet & bake for 15 to 20 mins.
- Serve!

Nutrition:

Calories 180, Carbohydrate 5g, Fat 6g, Sugar 2g, Protein 25g, Potassium 500mg, Sodium 280mg, Phosphorus 230mg

Land Main Courses

Chicken Breast with Lemon & Rosemary

Preparation time: 10 mins
Cooking time: 30 mins
Difficulty level: Medium
Serving: 1
PRAL: -2.3 (negative)

Ingredients:

- 4 boneless, skinless chicken breasts
- 1 tsp lemon juice
- 2-3 sprigs of fresh rosemary
- 2 tbsp olive oil
- Pepper to taste

Instructions:

- Preheat the oven to 375 degrees F.
- Season the chicken breast with pepper.
- Add olive oil into the intermediate skillet & heat it. Add chicken breast & sear for 2-3 mins per side. Add lemon juice over it.
- Transfer the skillet to the oven & bake for 20-25 mins.
- Serve!

Nutrition:

Calories 240, Carbohydrate 1g, Fat 14g, Sugar 0g, Protein 27g, Potassium 360mg, Sodium 100mg, Phosphorus 100mg

Beef Steaks with Mushroom Sauce

Preparation time: 10 mins
Cooking time: 10 mins
Difficulty level: Medium
Serving: 1
PRAL: -2.5 (negative)

Ingredients:

- 1 lb beef steaks
- 1 cup button mushrooms, sliced
- One tsp garlic, minced
- One tbsp fresh parsley, chopped
- One tsp pepper
- 1 tbsp olive oil

Instructions:

- Season the beef steak with pepper.
- Add olive oil into the decent skillet & heat it. Add beef steaks & cook for 3-4 mins per side.
- Remove the steak from the skillet.
- Add olive oil to the same pan & heat it. Add sliced mushrooms & garlic & sauté until tender.
- Season with pepper.
- Serve!

Nutrition:

Calories 250, Carbohydrate 3g, Fat 15g, Sugar 1g, Protein 25g, Potassium 500mg, Sodium 100mg, Phosphorus 100mg

Soups

Celery & Leek Soup

Preparation time: 15 mins
Cooking time: 30 mins
Difficulty level: Medium
Serving: 1
PRAL: -3.5 (negative)

Ingredients:

- 2 cups celery, chopped
- 2 cups leeks, sliced, white & light green parts only)
- 4 cups vegetable broth
- 2 tbsp olive oil
- Pepper, to taste

Instructions:

- Add olive oil into the pot & heat it.
- Add leeks & celery & sauté for 5-7 mins.
- Add vegetable broth & boil it. Reduce the heat & simmer & cook for 15 to 20 mins.
- Transfer the mixture to the blender & blend until smooth.
- Season with pepper.
- Serve!

Nutrition:

Calories 100, Carbohydrate 7g, Fat 7g, Sugar 2g, Protein 1g, Potassium 430mg, Sodium 130mg, Phosphorus 100mg

Cauliflower Soup with Turmeric & Ginger

Preparation time: 15 mins
Cooking time: 20 mins
Difficulty level: Medium
Serving: 1
PRAL: -3.8 (negative)

Ingredients:

- One head cauliflower, chopped
- One tbsp fresh ginger, minced
- 1 tsp turmeric powder
- 4 cups vegetable broth, low-sodium

Instructions:

- Add vegetable broth, turmeric, ginger, & cauliflower florets into the pot & boil it.
- Reduce the heat & cover the pot. Simmer for 15 to 20 mins.
- Transfer the mixture to the blender & blend until smooth.
- Return the pureed soup into the pot & heat it.
- Serve!

Nutrition:

Calories 50, Carbohydrate 8g, Fat 1g, Sugar 2g, Protein 2g, Potassium 360mg, Sodium 200mg, Phosphorus 60mg

Side Dishes

Baked Asparagus with Parmesan

Preparation time: 10 mins
Cooking time: 20 mins
Difficulty level: Medium
Serving: 1
PRAL: -2.6 (negative)

Ingredients:

- 1 bunch fresh asparagus
- 2 tbsp olive oil
- 2 tbsp parmesan cheese, grated
- Pepper to taste

Instructions:

- Preheat the oven to 425 degrees F.
- Rinse & trim the tough ends of the asparagus spears.
- Place the asparagus onto the baking sheet & drizzle with olive oil.
- Season with pepper.
- Bake for 15 to 20 mins.
- Serve!

Nutrition:

Calories 80, Carbohydrate 5g, Fat 6g, Sugar 0.5g, Protein 3g, Potassium 250mg, Sodium 100mg, Phosphorus 60mg

Sautéed Kale with Garlic & Chili

Preparation time: 10 mins
Cooking time: 10 mins
Difficulty level: Medium
Serving: 1
PRAL: -2.2 (negative)

Ingredients:

- 1 cup kale, washed & chopped
- 1 clove garlic, minced
- 1 fresh chili pepper, chopped
- 1 tbsp olive oil
- Pepper to taste

Instructions:

- Add olive oil into the skillet & heat it.
- Add minced garlic & chili pepper & cook for 1-2 mins.
- Add chopped kale & toss & fry for 3-5 mins.
- Season with pepper. Cook for 1-2 mins.
- Serve!

Nutrition:

Calories 80, Carbohydrate 8g, Fat 5g, Sugar 1g, Protein 2g, Potassium 320mg, Sodium 150mg, Phosphorus 45mg

Salads

Spinach Salad with Strawberries & Almonds

Preparation time: 10 mins
Cooking time: 0 mins
Difficulty level: Easy
Serving: 1
PRAL: -2.7 (negative)

Ingredients:

- 2 cups fresh spinach
- ½ cup strawberries
- 1 tbsp slivered almonds
- ½ tbsp olive oil

Instructions:

- Rinse & dry the spinach & strawberries.
- Add almonds, sliced strawberries, & spinach into the salad bowl & drizzle with olive oil. Toss well.
- Serve!

Nutrition:

Calories 100, Carbohydrate 9g, Fat 7g, Sugar 3g, Protein 2g, Potassium 300mg, Sodium 50mg, Phosphorus 60mg

Arugula Salad with Avocado & Walnuts

Preparation time: 10 mins
Cooking time: 0 mins
Difficulty level: Easy
Serving: 1
PRAL: -2.5 (negative)

Ingredients:

- 1 cup arugula
- Half ripe avocado, sliced
- ¼ cup of walnuts, chopped
- 1 tsp lemon juice
- 1 tbsp olive oil

Instructions:

- Add arugula, avocado, & walnuts into the salad bowl.
- Pour olive oil & lemon juice in another bowl & mix well.
- Add lemon mixture over salad. Toss well.
- Serve!

Nutrition:

Calories 220, Carbohydrate 9g, Fat 20g, Sugar 1g, Protein 3g, Potassium 372mg, Sodium 11mg, Phosphorus 75mg

Snacks:

Snacks

Cucumbers with Chickpea Hummus

Preparation time: 10 mins
Cooking time: 0 mins
Difficulty level: Easy
Serving: 1
PRAL: -2.9 (negative)

Ingredients:

- 1 cucumber
- ½ cup chickpeas, cooked
- 2 tbsp tahini
- 1 tsp lemon juice
- Pepper, to taste

Instructions:

- Add lemon juice, tahini, & cooked chickpeas into the blender & mix & mix.
- Rinse & peel the cucumber & cut into thin slices.
- Arrange the cucumber slices onto the plate.
- Add chickpea hummus in the middle.
- Serve!

Nutrition:

Calories 140, Carbohydrate 12g, Fat 7g, Sugar 1g, Protein 6g, Potassium 240mg, Sodium 150mg, Phosphorus 120mg

Roasted Almonds with Cinnamon

Preparation time: 5 mins
Cooking time: 12 mins
Difficulty level: Easy
Serving: 1
PRAL: -2.3 (negative)

Ingredients:

- 1 cup almonds
- 1 teaspoon cinnamon powder

Instructions:

- Firstly, preheat the oven to 350 degrees F.
- Place cinnamon powder & almonds into the mixing bowl & mix well.
- Spread this mixture onto the medium baking sheet & roast for 10-12 mins.
- Serve!

Nutrition:

Calories 180, Carbohydrate 6g, Fat 16g, Sugar 0g, Protein 6g, Potassium 207mg, Sodium 0mg, Phosphorus 137mg

Chocolate Mousse with Avocado

Preparation time: 5 mins
Cooking time: 0 mins
Difficulty level: Easy
Serving: 1
PRAL: -2.8 (negative)

Ingredients:

- 1 ripe avocado
- 2 tbsp unsweetened cocoa powder
- 2 tbsp sweetener

Instructions:

- Scoop out the flesh into the blender & mix together.
- Add sweetener & cocoa powder to the avocado into the blender & mix together.
- Serve!

Nutrition:

Calories 160, Carbohydrate 9g, Fat 14g, Sugar 1g, Protein 2g, Potassium 487mg, Sodium 4mg, Phosphorus 64mg

Vanilla Ice Cream with Fresh Strawberries

Preparation time: 30 mins
Cooking time: 0 mins
Difficulty level: Easy
Serving: 1
PRAL: -3.2 (negative)

Ingredients:

- 1 cup unsweetened Greek yogurt
- 1 tsp vanilla extract
- 1 cup fresh strawberries, sliced

Instructions:

- Add vanilla & Greek yogurt into the mixing bowl.
- Fold the strawberries into the yogurt mixture.
- Pour the mixture into the ice cream maker & churn according to the instructions.
- Freeze for 30 mins.
- Serve!

Nutrition:

Calories 120, Carbohydrate 10g, Fat 2g, Sugar 6g, Protein 10g, Potassium 180mg, Sodium 30mg, Phosphorus 100mg

Bonus Recipes Shopping List & 28 Days Meal Plan

Eggs	Cherry tomatoes	Parmesan cheese
Avocado	Pine nuts	Kale
Cheddar cheese	Mushrooms	Chili pepper
Black pepper	Walnuts	Spinach
Cucumber	Thyme	Strawberries
Spinach leaves	Tuna fillet	Almonds
Greek yogurt	Capers	Arugula
Lemon juice	Sole fillets	Chickpeas
Eggplant	Black olives	Tahini
Sun-dried tomatoes in oil	Chicken breasts	Almonds
Garlic	2 rosemary	Cinnamon powder
Olive oil	Beef steaks	Unsweetened cocoa powder
Zucchinis	Button mushrooms	Low-carb sweetener
Ricotta cheese	Celery	Unsweetened Greek yogurt
Mint leaves	Leeks	Vanilla extract
Shrimp	Vegetable broth	Fresh strawberries
Parsley leaves	Cauliflower	
Octopus	Ginger	
Fresh basil leaves	Turmeric powder	
	Fresh asparagus	

Week-1

	BREAKFAST	LUNCH	DINNER	SNACKS
MON	Mixed Vegetable Frittata Page: 15	Lentil and Tomato Soup Page: 28	Quinoa and Black Bean Burgers Page: 40	Cauliflower Gratin Page: 49
TUE	Whole Grain Crepes Page: 16	Zucchini Spaghetti with Avocado Pesto Page: 28	Roast Pork with Apple Sauce Page: 40	Lemon Asparagus Page: 50
WED	Oat Pancakes Page: 17	Spinach and Strawberry Salad Page: 29	Vegetable Minestrone Page: 43	Green Beans with Almonds Page: 50
THU	Avocado and Spinach Smoothie Page: 13	Risotto with Zucchini and Lemon Page: 23	Turkey Taco with Avocado Sauce Page: 38	Mashed Sweet Potatoes Page: 51
FRI	Blueberry Oatmeal Muffins Page: 13	Carrot Casserole Page: 31	Eggplant Cutlet with Mixed Salad Page: 38	Mushroom Stuffed Zucchini Page: 52
SAT	Baked Eggs with Avocado Page: 2	Baked Ratatouille Page: 32	Mushroom Stuffed Zucchini Page: 52	Couscous with Raisins and Almonds Page: 52
SUN	Cucumber and Spinach Smoothie Page: 2	Herb Risotto Page: 32	Seafood Salad with Avocado Page: 4	Hard Boiled Egg Page: 22

Week-2

	BREAKFAST	LUNCH	DINNER	SNACKS
MON	Yogurt with Berries and Chia Seeds Page: 14	Grilled Lemon Salmon Page: 33	Chickpea Pasta with Shrimp Page: 26	Chickpea Hummus Page: 22
TUE	Oatmeal Pancakes with Blueberry Sauce Page: 14	Cartoccio Trout with Aromatic Herbs Page: 34	Black Risotto with Squid and Peas Page: 27	Avocado Salsa with Corn Tortillas Page: 59
WED	Toast with Avocado and Cherry Tomatoes Page: 15	Salmon and Shrimp Skewers Page: 34	Zucchini Spaghetti with Anchovy Sauce Page: 27	Fresh Fruit Salad Page: 59
THU	Mixed Vegetable Frittata Page: 15	Baked Crab Meatballs Page: 36	Shrimp Tempura Page: 26	Cucumber Salad with Yogurt and Dill Page: 60
FRI	Quinoa and Red Fruits Porridge Page: 16	Fish Soup with Garlic Croutons Page: 37	Turkey Taco with Avocado Sauce Page: 38	Yogurt Sauce Page: 61
SAT	Whole Grain Crepes Page: 16	Vegan Sausages with Peperonata Page: 39	Cabbage Rolls with Wild Rice Page: 41	Guacamole with Corn Chips Page: 61
SUN	Sweet Potato Waffles Page: 17	Turkey Taco with Avocado Sauce Page: 38	Honey Glazed Pork Ribs Page: 42	Walnut and Blueberry Muffins Page: 62

Week-3

	BREAKFAST	LUNCH	DINNER	SNACKS
MON	Oat Pancakes Page: 17	Mushrooms Trifoliate Page: 21	Black Risotto with Squid and Peas Page: 27	Tuna Patties Page: 48
TUE	Avocado and Spinach Smoothie Page: 13	Risotto with Zucchini and Lemon Page: 23	Zucchini Spaghetti with Anchovy Sauce Page: 27	Spinach and Strawberry Salad Page: 29
WED	Quinoa and Red Fruits Porridge Page: 16	Quinoa and Shrimp Salad Page: 16	Risotto with Zucchini and Lemon Page: 23	Green Beans with Almonds Page: 50
THU	Whole Grain Crepes Page: 16	Fish Soup with Vegetables Page: 24	Lentil and Tomato Soup Page: 28	Beet and Walnut Salad Page: 53
FRI	Sweet Potato Waffles Page: 17	Zucchini Noodles Page: 25	Quinoa with Grilled Vegetables Page: 29	Avocado Stuffing Page: 20
SAT	Oat Pancakes Page: 17	Seafood Salad with Avocado Page: 26	Salmon and Shrimp Skewers Page: 34	Roman-Style Artichokes Page: 20
SUN	Cucumber and Spinach Smoothie Page: 2	Chickpea Pasta with Shrimp Page: 26	Cartoccio Trout with Aromatic Herbs Page: 34	Marinated Peppers Page: 21

Week-4

	BREAKFAST	LUNCH	DINNER	SNACKS
MON	Oat Pancakes Page: 17	Baked Crab Meatballs Page: 36	Cream of Pumpkin Soup Page: 44	Corn Soup Page: 46
TUE	Avocado and Spinach Smoothie Page: 13	Eggplant Cutlet with Mixed Salad Page: 38	Tuna Patties Page: 48	Tuna Patties Page: 48
WED	Yogurt with Berries and Chia Seeds Page: 14	Cabbage Rolls with Wild Rice Page: 41	Beef Steaks with Mushroom Sauce Page: 7	Cauliflower Gratin Page: 49
THU	Oatmeal Pancakes with Blueberry Sauce Page: 14	Honey Glazed Pork Ribs Page: 42	Chicken Breast with Lemon and Rosemary Page: 7	Mashed Sweet Potatoes Page: 51
FRI	Toast with Avocado and Cherry Tomatoes Page: 15	Vegetable Minestrone Page: 43	Baked Crab Meatballs Page: 36	Mushroom Stuffed Zucchini Page: 52
SAT	Mixed Vegetable Frittata Page: 15	Zucchini noodles Page: 25	Grilled Tuna with Lemon and Caper Sauce Page: 6	Beet and Mint Salad Page: 53
SUN	Quinoa and Red Fruits Porridge Page: 16	Lentil Soup Page: 44	Cartoccio Sole with Olives Page: 6	Brussels Sprout and Tangerine Salad Page: 57

Conversion Unit of Measurement

weight
(rounded to the nearest whole number)

IMPERIAL	METRIC
0.5 oz	14 g
1 oz	28 g
2 oz	58 g
3 oz	86 g
4 oz	114 g
5 oz	142 g
6 oz	170 g
7 oz	198 g
8 oz (1/2 lb)	226 g
9 oz	256 g
10 oz	284 g
11 oz	312 g
12 oz	340 g
13 oz	368 g
14 oz	396 g
15 oz	426 g
16 oz (1 lb)	454 g
24 oz (1 1/2 lb)	680 g

misc
(rounded to the closest equivalent)

IMPERIAL	
1 quart	4 cups (1 liter)
4 quarts	16 cups (4.5 liters)
6 quarts	24 cups (7 liters)
1 gallon	16 cups (4.5 liters)

volume
(rounded to the closest equivalent)

IMPERIAL	METRIC
1/8 tsp	0.5 mL
1/4 tsp	1 mL
1/2 tsp	2.5 mL
3/4 tsp	4 mL
1 tsp	5 mL
1 tbsp	15 mL
1 1/2 tbsp	25 mL
1/8 cup	30 mL
1/4 cup	60 mL
1/3 cup	80 mL
1/2 cup	120 mL
2/3 cup	160 mL
3/4 cup	180 mL
1 cup	240 mL

liquid
(rounded to the closest equivalent)

IMPERIAL	METRIC
0.5 oz	15 mL
1 oz	30 mL
2 oz	60 mL
3 oz	85 mL
4 oz	115 mL
5 oz	140 mL
6 oz	170 mL
7 oz	200 mL
8 oz	230 mL
9 oz	260 mL
10 oz	285 mL
11 oz	310 mL
12 oz	340 mL
13 oz	370 mL

temperature
(rounded to the closest equivalent)

IMPERIAL	METRIC
150 °F	65 °C
160 °F	70 °C
175 °F	80 °C
200 °F	95 °C
225 °F	110 °C
250 °F	120 °C
275 °F	135 °C
300 °F	150 °C
325 °F	160 °C
350 °F	175 °C
375 °F	190 °C
400 °F	205 °C
425 °F	220 °C
450 °F	230 °C
475 °F	245 °C
500 °F	260 °C

length
(rounded to the closest equivalent)

IMPERIAL	METRIC
1/8 inch	3 mm
1/4 inch	6 mm
1 inch	2.5 cm
1 1/4 inch	3 cm
2 inches	5 cm
6 inches	15 cm
8 inches	20 cm
9 inches	22.5 cm
10 inches	25 cm
11 inches	28 cm

INDEX

Conclusion

Dear Reader,

Thank you for placing your trust in me. I hope you enjoyed the book and the recipes but, in closing, I want to share you a message of encouragement.

I understand the daily challenges you face, but I also believe that every challenge brings new knowledge and opportunities. Never give up; continue your journey, and one day, you may find great satisfaction.

I hope this cookbook has made a positive impact on your daily life, even in a small way.

If you enjoyed it, I hope you will find time to leave me a positive review, I would really appreciate it. I would love to know what you enjoyed most about this book.

In my own small way, I can only wish you the best in life!

Emery Beckett

Printed in Great Britain
by Amazon